They Left; I Lived

A Boy Abandoned. A Silence That Shaped Him. A Man Who Rose.

By

Lou Dos Santos

ISBN: 978-1-923753-49-5

Published by:

LOU DOS SANTOS

Dedication

For my daughter,

May you never question your value in this world,
And may you always remember
That resilience is your inheritance.

Acknowledgement

This book was never written alone.

It was shaped by those who recognised something in me before I had the courage to see it myself.
It was strengthened by those who tested my resolve and, in doing so, fortified it.
And it was sustained by those who never stopped believing long after doubt had taken hold.

This story carries your fingerprints in every chapter.

Table of Contents

Prologue

The night my childhood ended wasn't stormy, no thunder cracked, nor did any spark of lightning split the sky. It was, in fact, disturbingly still. My mother's perfume clung to the air sweet, deliberate, and final. She didn't look back. Neither did he. The car door clicked shut with an indifference that would echo through the rest of my life.

I stood at the iron gates of the boarding school, clutching a suitcase too heavy for a twelve-year-old, packed not with clothes, but with the invisible weight of abandonment. I wanted to run and scream but children like me, quiet ones, odd ones, the ones who get left behind, we learn early that silence is safer than truth.

No one tells you that the absence of love leaves a louder void than the absence of sound.

But this isn't just a story of being left behind.

It is the story of how I discovered a second family within the same place I was banished to. This story is about how the bond I created with my found family, and the brutal code of brotherhood we forged, which taught me how to survive and ignite a life within me that no one could fathom.

From the dusty dormitories of apartheid-era South Africa to the glittering halls of global finance, this is the journey of a boy who was discarded and the man he chose to become.

They left; I lived.

And I'm here to tell the story.

Chapter 1:
The Night We Turned Back the Clock.

In the heart of Barberton, where the Makhonjwa Mountains stretch like the spines of sleeping giants and the earth whispers secrets in gold-dusted winds, stood the original Impala Hotel, a rickety monument to wild dreams and wilder nights. Nestled among the rugged hills of Mpumalanga's legendary landscape, it was less a hotel and more a boisterous heartbeat in the dusty chest of a frontier town.

The Impala was built from locally quarried stone and Oregan Pine, a type of wood that groaned like an old man's knees in winter. The building squatted proudly over the dirt road, its long wooden veranda watching over miners, gamblers, and drifters like a grizzled barkeep with stories too sad to tell and too good not to. The place catered to the kind of men who chased gold with more passion than wisdom, and often came away poorer but infinitely more interesting.

The saloon was the soul of the beast: dimly lit, heavy with the scent of sweat and smoke, and crowded with stories that had outgrown the men who told them. Oil lamps flickered along the cracked walls, casting dancing shadows over faded daguerreotypes of haunted-eyed prospectors and yellowing maps whose promises had long since expired. The floor, sticky with history and more than a little beer, creaked like it had opinions about your boots.

Every night, the room was filled with clinking glasses, belly laughs, and the occasional bar stool flying with a theatrical flair. Whisky flowed like the nearby streams: amber, fast, and untrustworthy. The piano, perpetually out of tune and only half-sober, tried its best to keep up.

Upstairs, modest guest rooms offered refuge to those too lucky or too broke to sleep elsewhere. Each one held a sagging iron bed that squealed in protest, a chipped porcelain basin that judged you silently, and a dresser that once belonged to someone's grandmother and smelled like it missed her. At the end of the hall, a communal bathroom boasted a copper tub so elegant, some claimed a prospector once tried to marry it.

Behind the building, the courtyard buzzed with life and smoke: horses stomping in stables, sparks flying from the blacksmith's forge, and men huddled by the fire pit, their eyes reflecting flames and fading dreams. Under a blanket of African stars, they spun tales with the solemnity of prophets, tales of nuggets the size of fists and losses too large for language.

But then came the fire.

It began as a small ember, perhaps with a misplaced match or an overambitious flambé attempt by the cook whose culinary genius leaned heavily on charred meat and wishful thinking. Fuelled by dry timber, alcohol, and years of poor decisions, the blaze tore through the Impala like it had a personal vendetta. By dawn, the proud old lady was gone, reduced to a skeletal frame of blackened beams and a lingering scent of ghosts.

Still, Barberton was made of grit and gold dust.

Not long after, a wealthy entrepreneur rumoured to have softer hands than a baby and a vision bolder than his neckties snatched up the scorched remains. Of course, he had no interest in miners or dented spittoons. This begs the question: Why did he invest? He invested because he saw something no one else did: opulence in the ashes. A phoenix with a monocle.

By the 1920s, the Impala had risen again, this time in pearls and perfume.

The new Impala Hotel was a colonial dream, draped in Art Deco silk. Its gleaming white façade sparkled under the African sun like a film star who'd seen too much but smiled anyway. Arched windows framed the horizon, wrought iron balconies curled with elegance, and the wooden trim whispered stories of its rough-hewn predecessor. Although faded, it still beamed as if mischievously winking to those who knew.

Inside, the lobby was all grace and grandeur. Teakwood floors shone like polished ambitions, high coffered ceilings gave room for dreams to echo, and European chandeliers spilled golden light like champagne. Plush Persian rugs muffled the footsteps of the powerful, and leather armchairs practically sighed when you sat in them. In the corner, a grand piano gleamed like it remembered every note the old one forgot.

The Gold Bar replaced the saloon, a lounge where spirits were now aged, not spilled. Bartenders wore bow ties, mixed cocktails with the seriousness of philosophers, and foraged locally for garnishes you could neither spell nor pronounce. The brawling was gone, replaced by a quieter kind of combat: the raising of eyebrows over trade deals and the subtle clink of old money.

The guest rooms now whispered luxury four-poster beds with linen that felt like sin, antique writing desks begging for confessions, clawfoot tubs that promised redemption, and balconies offering views too poetic to be accidental.

The stables gave way to a tea garden where roses blushed under gossiping bees and gazebos shaded lovers and liars alike. Beneath the hotel, the old gambling den became a wine cellar, a cool cavern of vintage South African pride, where miners' ghosts now swirled through bottles instead of smoke.

But the Impala, for all its elegance, never forgot.

In a quiet corner of the bar hangs a framed photograph: the original saloon in all its grimy, chaotic glory. No plaque or story, just a black-and-white whisper from the past, daring the present to pretend it came from somewhere else.

Some say that on certain nights, when the wind tiptoes through Barberton and the moon hangs low like a knowing eye, you can hear it.

A raspy laugh, drifting through the jasmine. The low thrum of an old piano, slightly off-key but sincere. A toast raised to luck, fate, and foolish men who believed in gold and gods in equal measure. And the clinking of glasses ghostly, merry, and echoing from a time when the floor creaked, the beer spilled freely, and the world still danced on the edge of discovery.

Chapter 2:
The Reunion at the Impala.

Tonight, the Impala Hotel wasn't a relic of Barberton's gilded past, but instead, pulsed with life, dressed to impress in its old bones and new varnish. The walls, which once soaked up the whisky-soaked confessions of miners and the mad dreams of fortune seekers, now stood straighter, as if keen to eavesdrop on a different kind of gathering.

The chandeliers flickered like they, too, remembered us, the boys we once were and the men we had become. Back then, we drank cola through chipped teeth and dreamt of Ferraris with rusted bicycles parked outside. Those days felt decades past. Now, we sipped aged whisky through crow's feet and prosthetic hips, and the dreams... well, they still showed up uninvited.

Some of us had traded hairlines for wisdom, others teeth for truth, and one or two had managed to hang on to both…bastards. But as I stepped beneath the amber glow of the antique chandelier, one thing rang clear: time might scuff the body, but it never truly dulls the spirit. Especially not when it's wrapped in the camaraderie of battle-hardened boyhood.

Aged wood and vintage charm wrapped around me like a tweed jacket I didn't know I'd missed. The scent of tobacco ghosts, old leather, and the faintest trace of expensive disappointment hit the senses like an old love letter never sent. A lazy jazz tune slinked through the air, curling around the room like a cat that knew it owned the place.

And then... *laughter*. Not the polite chuckle of boardroom survivors. No, this was the good stuff: deep, reckless, and entirely unfiltered, the kind of laughter that smuggled memory through the door and didn't bother knocking. It was the sound of firecrackers behind the gym, of curfews broken and math tests bombed, of dreams whispered by torchlight under mosquito nets.

I turned the corner, and there they were. Hendrik was the first to spot me, "Well, I'll be damned! If it isn't the pocket calculator with legs!"

"Still better looking than you remember," I fired back, stepping into a bear hug that cracked more vertebrae than a chiropractor on espresso.

"Gabriel!" Candice chimed, swooping in with that same mischievous grin she'd worn since Standard Five. "You still owe me five rand."

"I was twelve and under financial duress," I protested, mock-offended.

"Interest compounding daily since 1982," she winked.

We met in a chorus of backslaps and warm jabs; each embrace was a chapter in the unwritten book of our shared youth. There was no ceremony to it, just the instinctive, unspoken rhythm of people who had once mapped each other's lives in pencil and late-night whispers.

We spoke of the days when our greatest worries were looming math tests or sneaking into the kitchens for toast after lights-out. We laughed out loud, reminiscing of the nights when the world stretched before us like an empty canvas, waiting for our scribbles. Time had shaped us, moulded us, etched wrinkles where laughlines used to form, swapped lean muscle for soft bellies and stiff knees, but beneath it all, we were still those dreamers under the jacaranda trees.

The gilded ceiling of the Impala shimmered above us like a silent witness. It had seen miners, mayors, mischief-makers, and now it saw us older, yes, but not quite finished. Not quite tamed.

There was Hendrik, still the human landslide of laughter and loyalty. There was Candice, radiant as ever, with that sharp gaze that missed nothing and forgave most. And around us, the echo of memories stirred gently, like dust in sunlight. For a moment, the decades had melted, and in that moment, we were home.

The room erupted again, half laughter, half collective creaking of knees and memories.

We gathered beneath the gilded ceiling like a tribe returning from exile. In this half-renovated ballroom where bullet holes from a forgotten uprising still peeked out behind velvet drapes, we weren't strangers seasoned by time; we were the same misfits and rebels, now wrapped in linen shirts and reading glasses.

We raised our glasses, and with each clink, the years peeled back further.

"Remember when we tried to start a band?" someone asked.

"No one could sing, play, or even agree on a name for that matter," Hendrik noted.

"We were democratically dysfunctional," I added, laughing. "A metaphor for most of our adult lives."

Candice tapped her glass. "At least we agreed on one thing: never let Gabriel do the accounting. His idea of investment was lending five rand at 20% interest and calling it 'visionary banking.'"

"And look where that got me," I said with a mock bow. "A widow, a dodgy knee, and a name plaque at National Bank."

"Still," Hendrik said, his voice now gentler, "you were always the one who kept count not of money, but of people. Of who needed what. Of those who had no one else."

The laughter softened then, replaced by something quieter. Something shared. A coat of warmth had enveloped the entire table and its inhabitants

The truth was, I had built a family here, cobbled from the misfits of Barberton High School, patched together in rugby fields, detention halls, and stolen Sundays. When the world tossed me aside, these were the souls who picked me up, brushed me off, and told the world to shove it.

It wasn't blood that held us. Blood had vanished years ago, gone with the parents who dropped me at boarding school like a parcel they couldn't return.

No. This was something far more enduring. Trust forged in shared secrets. Survival cemented in loyalty. Love that never needed to be said aloud because it had already been proven in the thousand unspoken ways.

Tonight, the Impala shimmered not because of its brass chandeliers or restored Art Deco bar but because of what we brought into it: stories, scars, and the kind of unbreakable bond only time and tribulation can craft.

I looked around the room at the wild-haired girl who taught me to dance in the rain, the broad-shouldered boy who punched a prefect for calling me a freak, and the quiet one who shared his last slice of bread. In that moment, I knew: the real gold in Barberton was never buried beneath the hills. It was right here. Laughing, aging, and refusing to fade.

Glenn Smith: The Quiet Equation

Seated in a generously padded leather armchair, one leg folded neatly over the other, like a man who had nothing to prove (and plenty he could), Glenn Smith looked exactly like I remembered him: deliberate, composed, and built entirely from quiet contradictions. He hadn't changed much over the years, still spoke with the kind of economy that made philosophers look like gossip columnists, and still wore his silence like a bespoke suit.

As a boy, Glenn was the type who could dissolve into the background of a crowded dormitory like a well-behaved ghost. While we were out reenacting gladiator battles with hockey sticks, Glenn was calculating the probability of us breaking at least one limb, not because he cared to stop us, but because he found the math *interesting*.

You could say he was introspective, but that would be like calling the ocean *damp*.

He preferred numbers to people, logic to emotion, and diving headfirst into equations rather than into swimming pools, especially after that infamous poolside accident that left his legs scarred and his trust in aquatic environments permanently shaken. While the rest of us would have milked those injuries for sympathy and maybe a week off gym class, Glenn just limped quietly back to the maths club, as if pain were merely an unfortunate variable to be worked around.

His resilience wasn't the cinematic kind, the defiant chest-thumping of action heroes, but something far rarer. It was silent, uncomplaining, the kind of strength that bore weight without ever adjusting its posture. He never once said, *Look what I endured*. He simply endured, in silence.

And when he did speak, it was usually to explain Pythagoras with such elegance you'd think he'd invented the guy. Glenn didn't just solve equations; he *understood* them, coerced them to reveal their secrets with the quiet satisfaction of a man untangling a necklace knot with chopsticks. Others panicked at parabolas. Glenn? He invited them in for tea.

The son of a perennially absent doctor, he learned to fend for himself long before the rest of us had figured out how to boil an egg. He showed up to class clean, composed, and armed with more sharpened pencils than emotions. His academic success wasn't driven by ego, but by order. In a world full of messy feelings and hormonal chaos, equations offered him something comforting: a right answer.

And yet, for all his detachment, Glenn *noticed* things. Not in a flashy, Sherlock Holmes kind of way, but in the quiet, deliberate way someone notices you're about to cry and hands you a tissue without saying a word.

He was my roommate, my tutor, and my accidental guru, all in one. While others saw a socially awkward number-muncher, I saw the man who taught me how to memorise formulas with photographic precision, who coached me through trigonometry by comparing it to music chords, and who, perhaps most importantly, never once made me feel stupid.

He gave his time, knowledge, and his calm steadiness without ever expecting applause. Glenn didn't need recognition, but I needed to give it.

So, when the world eventually tossed me a sliver of fortune, my first house, I did what felt right. I gave it to Glenn.

He blinked. "That's irrational," he said flatly.

"Like the square root of two," I replied.

He allowed the corner of his mouth to quirk upward, which was basically a standing ovation, by Glenn's standards.

Years had passed since then. He built a quiet life, as dignified and unassuming as the man himself. But I couldn't stand the thought of his brilliance going unnoticed forever. So, I pulled a few strings, whispered in a few strategic ears, and made sure the right people saw what I'd always seen: a mind sharper than most and a soul even rarer.

Eventually, I maneuvered him into academia, not just as a professor, but as Dean of the local university. It wasn't easy. Glenn resisted the whole way.

"I'm not suited for leadership," he insisted.

"That's exactly why you should lead," I said.

He paused. "That's logically inconsistent."

"Welcome to humanity."

Although still a bit uneasy, he accepted. And, unsurprisingly, he thrived. Not because he craved authority, but because the students saw what I had seen: a quiet giant who didn't seek to be heard, but who always had something worth hearing. He didn't command respect, he *earned* it, one thoughtful pause and perfectly timed insight at a time.

Glenn never chased the spotlight. But in the end, it found him anyway, not with fanfare, but with reverence. And as I watched him shape the next generation with the same gentle brilliance that once reshaped my own world, I realised something simple but profound:

Some people lead with fire.

Others, like Glenn, lead with light.

And while fire burns bright, it's the quiet light that helps us find our way in the dark.

Pieter and Willem: Symmetry in Chaos

Not far from where Glenn held court with his quiet gravitas, two figures stood conspicuously under what appeared to be an oversized rubber plant, possibly hiding from someone or, more likely, observing. Their hair was the same shade of controlled chaos, their shirts identically wrinkled, and their eyes alight with that unmistakable gleam of impending mischief. Pieter and Willem: the twins.

Still indistinguishable. Still inseparable. Still very much... *themselves*.

Even now, after decades and dubious facial hair experiments, it was as if someone had copied and pasted them into adulthood without changing the original file. They moved like a mirrored set of marionettes if marionettes could calculate quantum drift while fixing a coffee machine using parts from a lawnmower.

They had always operated with the eerie synchronicity of a single consciousness distributed across two bodies. If you spoke to one, the other finished the sentence; ask a question, and you received an answer in stereo. It was charming. It was disturbing. Somehow, it was always funny.

They came from modest beginnings. Two scrappy lads dropped into the world of boarding school like astronauts onto a strange planet. While others disappeared home for the holidays, the twins remained, custodians of the empty halls and their echoing curiosity. They made the school their laboratory, their workshop, their jungle gym of discovery.

Their dorm room 3B, top floor, perpetually smelling of ozone and burnt toast, had once featured a hand-painted sign that read: *Abandon Common Sense, All Ye Who Enter Here*. Inside, chaos reigned. Coils of copper wire, half-disassembled radios, jars filled with suspiciously glowing liquids, some of which occasionally *hummed*, were scattered throughout. There were beakers that boiled without heat, petri dishes labelled "Don't Open Unless You Have a Spare Week," and at least one ceiling tile still missing from the time they attempted to make it rain indoors.

Their favourite prank? Reprogramming the school bell to play Mozart's *Requiem* in D minor. At midnight. For a week.

However, behind the smoke, sparks, and disciplinary letters, their brilliance was blinding. They could teach kinetic energy better than any textbook, using only a slingshot, a grapefruit, and an unsuspecting prefect. Biology, chemistry, physics, they deconstructed it all, then rebuilt it in ways that made even the most disinterested student lean forward in fascination.

I still remember them helping me survive biology, turning photosynthesis into a kind of absurd poetry, complete with interpretive dance. They had no patience for ego, but all the time in the world for curiosity. They didn't hoard knowledge; they broadcast it like rogue radio towers, tuned into the frequency of wonder.

And so, when life finally gave me the means to give something back, I founded *The Twinn Foundation,* named, of course, with two *n*s. It was more than a nod to them. It was a mission.

The Foundation became a global movement, dedicated to nurturing the same spirit of boundless experimentation and ethical exploration that had once spilled across their dorm floor. It funds research labs, hosts competitions for young inventors, and even offers scholarships to students who've been caught trying to microwave glassware because brilliance, like beakers, sometimes breaks before it shines.

Pieter and Willem, as ever, refused to take credit. "We just like making stuff go boom," Pieter said.

"With proper safety goggles," Willem added.

And yet, the world now knew their names not because they asked to be seen, but because they made the rest of us see differently.

They taught me and all of us that curiosity is the most contagious kind of magic. That wonder is worth cultivating. And that true genius often comes with burn marks, mismatched socks, and a twin who won't stop humming Bach.

Monica Coetzee: Polished to Perfection

Standing just beyond the symmetrical chaos of the twins, beneath the forgiving glow of an antique chandelier, was Monica Coetzee, effortless, poised, and eternally composed. She didn't need to command attention. She *curated* it.

The daughter of an old-money asbestos dynasty (before the lawsuits, naturally), Monica wore wealth like she wore her perfume, elegantly, sparingly, and only noticeable when you were close enough to ask, *what is that?* She didn't flaunt, but floated. Everything about her whispered understated luxury, from her patent leather shoes always the exact shade of the season to the way her ponytails swayed with perfect symmetry, as if choreographed by a discreet team of stylists hiding in the wings.

She was tall, immaculately dressed, with glasses that made her look just brainy enough to make teachers nervous and boys stammer. And then there were the bangles. Dozens of them, stacked on each wrist like miniature chandeliers, never clashing, never accidental. They sang before she did. You could always hear Monica coming. Not like thunder. Like wind chimes.

"Here comes Monica," the corridors whispered.

Some girls projected confidence. Monica projected a finish. If your tie was crooked, your hem untucked, your life even slightly askew, she would fix it with the same calm efficiency you'd use to pluck lint from velvet. She never asked or waited. She simply *restored*. She was, quite unapologetically, my groomer.

No, not in the sinister, headline-worthy sense. I mean the kind who would reach over, mid-conversation, to flatten your collar or discreetly de-fluff your blazer. Morning assembly was a parade, and thanks to Monica, I never arrived looking like a crumpled footnote.

"Stand still," she'd say, in that lightly amused tone, brushing invisible dust from my lapel as if rescuing me from social extinction. I never thanked her. That was part of the unspoken contract. Gratitude would have ruined the ritual.

While most of us *lived* at the school, Monica only *visited*. Every Friday, a chauffeur-driven black sedan would appear like clockwork, collecting her for a weekend filled with garden luncheons, art galleries, and family functions where names were double-barrelled, and silverware came in *sets*. She returned each Sunday with tales of places we'd only seen in magazines, her suitcase smelling faintly of bergamot and privilege.

But never once did she boast. If anything, her wealth seemed like a background track she couldn't quite mute. It was *there*, yes, but not the whole song.

She was always smiling, always laughing, the kind of laugh that sparkled but never cracked. And yet, beneath all that glossy serenity, you sometimes got the feeling she wasn't just *polished,* she was *armoured.* Whether her joy was real or part of the presentation, no one dared ask. Some stories, after all, weren't meant to be unpacked.

Naturally, the world tried to catch up with Monica, but she stayed one step ahead, bangles chiming in time. She took her gift, her compulsive need to perfect and steered it straight into Hollywood.

Not as an actress, mind you. Monica had never needed the spotlight to shine. She became a stand-in artist, a behind-the-scenes miracle worker for some of the biggest names in cinema. The kind of woman who could make a Dior gown drape like a waterfall, or who'd nudge the key light by two degrees and suddenly *bam* the cheekbone was a poem.

She adjusted waistlines, polished diamonds, and redirected wind machines. She could spot a mascara smudge from twenty paces and solve it without smearing a single emotion. In a town built on illusion, Monica didn't just maintain the magic; she *made* it seamless.

While the credits rolled and the red carpets were rolled up, Monica remained invisible. But every detail that dazzled, every moment that felt just a little too perfect? That was Monica's doing.

The girl who once smoothed my collar now smoothed the stars.

And somehow, she still never asked for thanks.

Candice Nel: The Quiet Flame

Candice Nel stood in a quiet corner, half-shadowed by a velvet curtain and the soft flicker of wall sconces. She was talking to Hendrik, conversing with an effortless grace, as if they met every day. The years that had stretched between them simply folded away, like the pages of a book reopening to a favourite chapter.

Their laughter came in intervals, hers light and melodic, his deep and gravelly, like an old record player warming up. It was the sound of shared history, of inside jokes weathered by time and made better by distance. Hendrik leaned slightly closer than necessary, his grin tugging at one corner of his mouth in that way that always preceded a story he'd have to censor halfway through.

Candice still carried herself with the same unshakable ease she'd always had. Confidence didn't cling to her; it radiated from her, soft and self-assured. Her presence was never loud, but somehow undeniable like the scent of rain on hot stone, or the quiet certainty of sunrise.

She spoke with warmth and just the right amount of mischief, her eyes constantly scanning not just the room, but *beneath* it, reading people the way others read body language or poorly hidden emotions. Hendrik, grounded as ever in his well-cut jacket and polished boots, listened with the reverence of someone who understood the value of someone like her. Their lives had taken different highways, hers toward quiet rebellion, his toward dutiful order, but the thread between them remained untangled, steady, and intact.

In those few shared moments, time bent slightly. They weren't middle-aged professionals laughing politely at reunions. They were once again those two teenagers under the jacaranda trees, sharing stolen sweets and imagined futures, dreaming of everything and afraid of nothing.

Candice had always been a mystery wrapped in clarity. She didn't need to raise her voice or outshine anyone to be seen. She made her impact in subtler ways in sideways glances, in the steadiness of her walk, in the way she took up space not with arrogance, but with certainty.

She hadn't been abandoned as I had; she'd been *exiled*. Sent away, not for failing, but for refusing to be small. Her family wanted her refined, contained, predictable. But Candice carved out her space inside the cold stone halls of boarding school like water in rock, slow, persistent, undeniable.

And somehow, in the middle of all that, she saw *me*.

Not as a cause. Not as a project. But simply, clearly.

There were no grand declarations. No orchestrated rescues. Just quiet gestures: a bruised apple placed beside me when I hadn't eaten. A perfectly timed glance during assembly that said, *You've got this*. She never offered pity; it would have insulted us both. Instead, she offered something much rarer: *presence*.

When I struggled with reading when letters danced on the page like cruel jokes, she never told me I was smart "in other ways." She just said, "Your brain's wired differently. That's not a bad thing. Might even be a *better* thing."

And suddenly, I wasn't broken. I was just *different*. And difference, in her world, didn't require an apology.

Then came *that* day.

The boys pack-minded, insecure, drunk on their own juvenile cruelty, pushed too far. A shove. A laugh. A staircase. I remember the humiliation more than the pain.

And there she was.

First on the scene. Not flustered. Not panicked. Just *present*. She didn't scream or throw fists. She didn't need to. Her voice measured, sharp as polished steel, cut through their noise like a scalpel.

She dismantled them with a surgeon's grace. Not with threats or insults, but with truths so precise they left no room for rebuttal. Cowards, she called them. Predictable, insecure cowards who only felt strong in groups and only laughed when someone else bled. They scattered like leaves in the wind.

And then, she turned to me.

No pity. No exaggerated concern. Just that trademark sigh of hers, half bemusement, half disappointment and a dry, teasing: "You do realise that staircase wasn't part of the curriculum?"

I laughed through the sting. Of embarrassment. Of bruises. Of *being seen*.

She offered me her hand not to rescue me, but to remind me I didn't have to stand alone.

After that day, something shifted. The others left me alone. And Candice? She never brought it up again. But from then on, she walked just slightly slower beside me, sat a little closer in class, and said just enough to make the world feel navigable. She didn't fix me, because she knew that she didn't need to. She just made space for me to be exactly who I was and helped me believe that space was mine to take.

When I look back on those days, I don't remember the teachers who looked away, or the boys who tried to shatter what was already fragile.

I remember her: steady, fierce, disarmingly kind, and completely unforgettable.

Hendrik: The Unbreakable Anchor

There were big people, then there were strong people, and then there was Hendrick.

You couldn't miss him if you tried. He was the kind of presence who could be seen ten seconds before he entered the room. Big, broad-shouldered, built like a rugby scrum in human form, with a mane of unruly curls that defied gravity and grooming alike. His shirt sleeves were always half-rolled, his tie permanently askew, and there was usually a smudge of paint or grease somewhere on him, proof that he'd been building, fixing, *doing* something with those impossible hands.

And then there was *that* laugh.

It started as a snort, turned into a growl, and ended somewhere between a honk and a roar. It echoed down corridors and around corners, ricocheted off chapel walls and dormitory ceilings. It shook windows. It startled pigeons. It was *alive*. The boys called him "The Pig" not cruelly, but with affection, reverence even. His laugh wasn't noise. It was *medicine,* the kind that healed bruised egos and chased away loneliness.

However, behind all the decibels and the slap-on-the-back charisma was something deeper. Something *solid*.

Hendrik had the kind of gravity that held things in place. Misfits, stragglers, kids with unspoken hurts, we orbited around him without ever having to ask why. However, he didn't posture or preach. He was just a walking fortress of good humour and unshakeable loyalty.

If a prefect sneered, Hendrik stepped between you. If a bully shoved, Hendrik was already there, not with fists, but with presence. And if fists were ever needed, well, let's just say no one *ever* needed to ask twice.

He came from simple roots. His father, for example, drove the early morning train that rattled between cities; this daily rhythm of whistles and steel-on-steel became the soundtrack of Hendrik's boyhood. While the world slept, his mother shaped bread, her hands kneading dough while her son figured out how to mend a broken bicycle chain with a paperclip and prayer.

They rarely crossed paths. His parents were shadows moving in opposite directions, passing each other with a nod and a tired kiss. He had five siblings, some older, some younger, but at school, they were more myth than memory. Ask Hendrik about them, and he'd shrug: *"They're around."* As if that was enough. As if *he* were enough.

Most boys went home on weekends to roast dinners, family fights, and laundry done by someone else. Hendrik stayed. Quietly. Consistently. Holidays, too. And when everyone else chased sun and surf, he patched dorm windows, painted handrails, rewired the AV room after someone (possibly the twins) blew the fuse trying to microwave a frog's heart.

His hands were always busy fixing what was broken, building what others didn't notice needed building. It was his way of making order in a world that offered him none.

For all his volume, Hendrik carried a deep, almost sacred sense of duty. The world had never owed him anything, and he never expected it to. But once you had his loyalty (a rare currency), he'd walk through fire for you and somehow, make it fun. He'd curse the flames, laugh through the smoke, and probably hand you a screwdriver halfway through the blaze.

He was not flawless. He forgot birthdays. He borrowed tools without returning them. He once attempted to build a rocket from a fire extinguisher and half a chemistry set. (It didn't reach space, but it *did* reach the roof.)

But he was *good.* He was solid and uncomplicated, in a way that didn't announce itself, and somewhere between Candice's fierce, quiet rebellion and Hendrik's riotous loyalty, I found something I didn't know I needed: *Belonging.* Not the kind built on shared hobbies or bloodlines, but belonging built on being *seen* and *chosen* by people who didn't need to save you. Just stand beside you.

Chapter 3:
Where The Story Begins.

It seemed like everyone had developed an uncanny fascination with my so-called "life success," as if my transformation from anxious schoolboy to supposedly influential banker had been part of some grand, well-executed plan. In reality, it was far more accidental a parade of questionable choices, blind luck, and sheer stubborn momentum masquerading as strategy.

As a boy, I'd all but folded into the back row of classrooms, certain that drawing attention would summon disaster. Now, people whispered as I passed as if success were a cloak I'd draped over myself rather than a patchwork quilt sewn together through trial and error.

If my life were a documentary, it wouldn't be one of those glossy motivational reels with swelling strings and inspirational voiceovers. No, mine would be a dark comedy, narrated with dry sarcasm and punctuated by awkward miracles: a montage of wrong doors opened, risks taken for the wrong reasons, and near-catastrophes that somehow turned out alright. Think less *rise to glory* and more *how did we get here, and why is the furniture on fire?*

People love to romanticise success, as if it's a straight road paved with clean intentions and well-timed sacrifices. Mine, however, was more like a maze designed by a sleep-deprived drunk with a grudge, confusing, convoluted, and marked by occasional trapdoors.

And yet, here I am.

Maybe what fascinates people isn't the success itself, but the sheer improbability of it. The fact that the boy who used to hoard coins in hidden sock-drawer banks, terrified of theft and loss, somehow ended up managing vaults and balance sheets that could fund small nations. The irony is so rich, I'd laugh if I weren't still mildly bewildered by it.

If you'd asked thirteen-year-old me what I hoped for, he probably would've shrugged and muttered something about staying out of trouble and maybe keeping his allowance intact. He wouldn't have imagined this, a world of fine suits, long boardroom tables, and a currency of confidence that took years to counterfeit convincingly.

So, when people lean in with glimmering curiosity and ask, *How did you do it?*, I can't help but smile. Because, honestly? I have no earthly idea, but oh, what a ride it has been.

Drinks ordered, we migrated to the garden behind the Impala, well-manicured, lantern-lit, and wrapped in the scent of fresh earth and blooming memory. We settled into a wide circular sofa that cradled us in effortless ease, old friends sinking into old rhythms. The murmur of conversation laced itself with the soft trickle of a nearby fountain, while birdsong, the occasional laugh, and the clink of ice in glasses composed an impromptu symphony of reunion.

Overhead, the sky melted into shades of amber and lavender, and for a moment, the evening held its breath.

The Impala Hotel stood just beyond the garden wall, unchanged in its quiet majesty. A monument to our youth. Its polished stone paths and glowing windows whispered of dormitory confessions, scrapes and schemes, and footsteps too fast for discipline. It had seen our beginnings, now it held the echoes of who we'd become.

I traced the cool rim of my glass and let my gaze drift between the now and the then. The people around me had been the background music of my formative years, and somehow, here we all were again. Weathered. Wiser. Somewhat creakier. And yet, not so far from the kids we once were.

The laughter softened. The stories deepened.

And then Hendrik stood.

Of course it was Hendrik. With that presence, half earthquake, half shepherd and a twinkle in his eye that always warned of incoming disruption.

He let his gaze sweep the group before finally landing on me.

"Your life's been fascinating," he said, with the practised understatement of someone dropping a grenade in a tearoom.

Then he locked eyes with me. "You should write a book."

I blinked. "What? Me?" I laughed, shaking my head. "My life's boring."

But even as I said it, something shifted. Quietly. Persistently.

The idea settled beside me like an old acquaintance. Maybe it was the timing, retirement now a certainty, the noise of boardrooms behind me, the quiet ahead suddenly vast and full of unwritten possibility.

There were stories. So many, in fact. Some were glorious; others, however, were not so much. Admittedly, a few were too painful to say aloud; nevertheless, all of them were true. Ultimately, perhaps truth, especially the complicated, contradictory kind, is worth sharing.

We parted that evening with hugs and promises, plans to meet at the school the next morning. But as I walked to my room, my mind was already somewhere else. Not in the present, but buried in boxes of memory I hadn't opened in years.

By the time I turned the key, the synopsis was already forming uninvited, but not unwelcome.

And so, this story begins where I thought it had ended, not in a boardroom, at the altar or the graveside, but on a quiet street. I arrived with nothing but a suitcase and a soul stitched together by everything I'd lost.

And still, somehow, I felt lighter than I had in years.

This isn't the story of a man who conquered the world.

It's the story of a boy who was left behind and the winding, improbable journey he took to find his way back.

I don't offer wisdom, only experience.

I don't promise answers, only moments, some painful and so that they still live just beneath my skin, while others just plain absurd.

But every one of them is true.

Maybe Hendrik was right. Maybe it's worth telling not because it's grand, but because it's ordinary. Because it's made of detours, failures, lucky breaks, second chances, and lessons earned the hard way.

Because I stumbled through like everyone else, sometimes holding on by a thread, sometimes celebrating victories I didn't realise were victories until much later.

And maybe just maybe that's enough.

Chapter 4:
Born in the Shadows. Born for Adventure.

Let's rewind to a freezing winter night in the early fifties, in a Portuguese village so small it barely showed up on the postman's map. That's where I made my debut, christened with solemn flair as *Gabriel Duarte Almeida*. Sounds noble, doesn't it? Trust me. The name was the only thing remotely grand about that night.

The hospital had all the ambience of a haunted house designed by communist architects. Paint peeled from the walls like burned parchment, the lights flickered in Morse code ("Run... while... you... can"), and the metal beds creaked like they knew secrets they wished they could forget.

The nurses? Women carved from granite, with the dead-eyed expressions of those who had long since stopped believing in miracles and possibly moonlighted as exorcists.

In the middle of this gothic opera, my mother laboured on, her expression somewhere between martyrdom and homicide. Beside her stood my aunt, a nurse at the hospital and a certified specialist in inappropriate humour during medical emergencies.

The Birth of a Legend (According to Me)

Aunt: "So, you ready to pop this one out, or should we wait until spring?"

Mother: *groans,* "I swear, if you don't stop, I'm naming him after you."

Aunt: *gasps* "Ooh, 'Aunt Gabriel' that has a certain elegance, don't you think?"

And so, between sarcasm and contractions, with one final, theatrical groan and a symphony of Portuguese profanities that made the attending priest retreat, I entered stage left. Let's be clear: I was never going to arrive quietly.

The hospital resembled a horror film set, the night was cold enough to make penguins question their life choices, and there I was, wailing like a soap opera cliffhanger. According to legend, the lights dimmed dramatically. Somewhere, a nurse fainted. The walls recoiled.

I was not what you'd call a "cute baby." Family folklore describes me as a cross between a monkey and a slightly bruised potato. The sort of newborn that made relatives tilt their heads and offer compliments with the uncertainty usually reserved for modern art.

"Oh, how... *precious*," one might have said, voice cracking under the strain of diplomacy.

"Yes, very... strong-looking," another added, with a nod that was clearly meant for emotional support.

"Indeed... robust," someone else managed, eyes slightly widened.

And in the corner, my grandmother silently crossed herself.

Fast forward two years.

Enter my brother, blond, blue-eyed, glowing like an advertisement for angelic genetics. He looked like he belonged on the cover of *Baby Vogue* (if that existed), while I resembled the before picture in a miracle cream ad.

My early years were unconventional. When I wasn't brawling with my brother or staging impromptu mixed martial arts bouts with the neighbour kids, I lived a secret life... as a diplomat.

Beneath the grand oak desk in our study, I held court with my loyal subjects: the teddies. Yes, teddies. Sir Whiskers. Count Snugglebottom. Baron Fuzzington. Each had a title, a teacup, and a position in my fuzzy parliament.

While the other boys collected scars like merit badges, I arranged seating charts for Bear Summits and managed sugar bowl territorial disputes like a mini Versailles.

It was all top secret. If my brother found out, I'd be socially executed before recess.

Then came *the Incident.*

Mid-negotiation, Sir Whiskers and Count Snugglebottom were clashing over nap protocol, and disaster struck: My mother walked in. When she barged in, there was a moment where both she and I froze up. Everyone froze except Sir Whiskers, who tipped into the sugar bowl with all the grace of a drunken diplomat.

She blinked, "What on earth are you doing under there?" she asked, her voice a perfect cocktail of curiosity and existential alarm.

"Nothing!" I squeaked, flinging Count Snugglebottom behind my back like contraband.

She raised a single eyebrow, a maternal weapon of mass destruction marking the end of the conversation, or so I thought.

Three days later, over breakfast, she struck with surgical precision. Between buttering toast and sipping tea, she said, "You know… boys usually play with cars, not teddies."

I nearly inhaled my cornflakes. It was so casual, so devastating, so expertly timed. It landed with the emotional weight of a Shakespearean monologue performed in slow motion.

From that moment on, I launched a campaign, a *Manhood Reclamation Initiative.*

"I want a Porsche," I declared with all the fire of a six-year-old trying to rewrite fate.

She didn't blink. Just sipped her tea as if she'd been expecting it since the womb, and a few days later, the universe delivered.

Well, sort of. She handed me a *plastic Porsche.* Brown. Possibly cursed. The kind of toy that looked like it had been rejected by a garage sale and run over by a metaphor.

It squeaked.

Constantly.

Not a noble squeak. Not even a whimsical one. This was a *death-rattle squeak*, like a rubber duck having an existential crisis.

I paraded that thing for three glorious hours before my mother, the guardian of silence and sanity, snapped, and with the precision of a javelin thrower, she snatched the Porsche and launched it into the driveway.

Boom.

The Porsche exploded into a hundred tiny pieces. I stood there, betrayed. Shattered. All that remained was the echo of a squeak and the burning resolve of a vendetta.

I narrowed my eyes.

"One day," I vowed, "I'm going to buy a *real* Porsche. And we'll see if you can throw *that* one."

Years later….

Fast forward twenty-two years.

The prophecy was fulfilled.

I was now a sharply dressed executive banker in Cape Town. And yes, I had my Porsche, a sleek, silver, humming like temptation on wheels, and with more buttons than a NASA cockpit.

I hadn't spoken to my mother in decades. But something stirred a nostalgic pang, subtle yet insistent. A longing not for reconciliation, but for recognition. A need to whisper across the years: *Look, Ma. No teddies.*

Enter Jessie: beautiful, effortless, like a summer breeze that knows it doesn't need permission to turn heads.

She was in town for a fortnight, between tennis tournaments and the blur of airports. We did all the things young, successful executives and lovers do to feel vividly, foolishly alive, lingering over wine at Stellenbosch estates where the air smelled of oak and ambition, cruising down Clarence Drive with the sea keeping pace like a faithful accomplice, and debating, with far too much passion, whether oysters had emotions or were just tragically misunderstood molluscs.

Then came the moment.

We pulled over at Lagoon Beach. The wind was theatrical, and the light, golden. I asked Jessie to pose on the bonnet because nothing says poetic justice like a Porsche, a mini-skirt, and a camera with good lighting.

The skirt, by the way, wasn't so much short as theoretical. It had ambitions of being clothing, but mostly functioned as a suggestion.

Click.

I printed the photo. Scrawled a note, *"Living in Cape Town. Here's the address."*

Posted it. No frills. Just facts.

Weeks passed.

Then it arrived.

A single postcard. No greeting. No preamble.

Just one line, written in her razor-sharp handwriting:

"Couldn't you have gotten something in brown?"

I stared at it.

No warmth. No signature. Just *that.*

Then I flipped it over.

PS: "Well… beats playing with teddies, I suppose."

And I swear I heard her smirk from 1,400 kilometres away.

Just like that, she reclaimed the upper hand. Decades of ambition, degrees, breakups, and bank statements, and she undid me with two sentences and a postcard.

That was the last I heard from her.

Because in the great chess game of life, no matter how many luxury cars you buy or photos you pose for…

You never, *ever*, beat a mother armed with wit, memory, and excellent stationery.

Chapter 5:
A Comedy of Waves and Wanderlust.

In the 1960s, the Portuguese government actively encouraged migration to its African colonies, particularly Angola and Mozambique, as part of its colonial strategy under the Estado Novo regime. These territories were seen as economically promising and politically strategic, offering fertile land, mineral wealth, and expanding urban centres that promised opportunity for settlers. The influx was intended to reinforce Portuguese control, both by developing industries like coffee, cotton, and mining, and by physically countering growing nationalist movements such as MPLA and FRELIMO.

However, the settler experience proved far from idyllic. Many Portuguese emigrants, especially those from poorer rural backgrounds, were met with environmental hardships, cultural isolation, and increasing instability as resistance to colonial rule intensified. By the late 1960s and early 1970s, escalating anti-colonial conflict made life in the colonies increasingly dangerous, turning initial dreams of prosperity into a precarious existence amid political unrest and looming decolonisation.

***

Let's rewind to the first major plot twist of my young life, the moment everything shifted without warning, like the sudden lurch of a ship pulling out of harbour. I was still a kid, blissfully unaware that my family had decided to pack up our lives and emigrate to Africa. It was, in fact, all cloak-and-dagger stuff; there was no family meeting and no globe-pointing explanation. Instead, one day, out of the blue, my mother emerged from a back room, dragging a massive trunk that looked like it had last seen service in a 19th-century expedition.

Inside? Not treasure. Clothes. Handmade clothes. And not just a few tasteful pieces. No! This was a full-blown textile explosion. Shorts, shirts, sleeveless sweaters, and sandals all stitched with the kind of commitment that suggested my mother had mistaken our upcoming journey for a year-long safari-themed fashion show.

"Why no winter clothes?" I asked, eyeing the pile of sun-soaked optimism.

"You're going to Africa," she said, with the air of someone revealing a twist ending. "It's hot there."

And that was that. No follow-up. No context. Just a casual dispatch that our continent was changing, and apparently so was my climate.

Months later, I stood in the heart of some remote African outpost, sandals on feet, knees knocking, breath visible as snowflakes pirouetted around me like confetti at the world's most ironic joke: A snowstorm. In Africa.

There I was, dressed for a beach barbecue, teeth chattering like castanets, as I watched snow settle onto my bare arms with theatrical delicacy.

"So much for it being hot," I muttered through frozen lips, each snowflake a frosty little postscript to my mother's climate forecast.

Life, I was beginning to learn, had a wicked sense of humour, and mine was only just getting started.

And so, there I was aboard what could only be described as a floating antique shop with engine trouble. Our so-called steamship didn't sail so much as wheeze its way across the Atlantic, groaning with each nautical mile like an asthmatic elephant competing in an ultramarathon. It wasn't a voyage; it was an endurance test with prizes in seasickness and spiritual disillusionment.

As for me, I resembled a Boy Scout who had been mugged by a haberdashery on its last legs. My outfit, curated by a loving but fashionably vengeful mother, consisted of hand-stitched wool and twine arranged in what I can only describe as postcolonial chaos couture. My sandals flapped mournfully with each step, like ducks startled mid-yawn. My socks clung to my calves with the panic of a bad idea mid-regret. And the shirt? Stiff as ship canvas, and itchy as betrayal, the shirt scratched in places I hadn't even mapped out anatomically. Even the seagulls above joined the critique, circling like airborne fashion editors, cackling in what I'm certain was derisive seagull laughter.

Our noble vessel, if nobility can be defined by creaking joints and terminal rust, looked like it had once been a museum exhibit titled, *Maritime Mistakes of the Early 20th Century*. Its hull was a patchwork quilt of dents and decay, its lifeboats looked like they'd rather sink than serve, and every pipe exhaled with the heavy sigh of a pensioner being asked to run a triathlon. The ship didn't simply move; rather, it convulsed. Each wave prompted a full-body groan, as if the ocean had hurled a personal insult at its ancestry. Furthermore, it smelled perpetually of damp wood, overboiled cabbage, and the sweet melancholy of dreams deferred.

The passengers were a cocktail of wide-eyed naiveté and misguided colonial enthusiasm. Young couples paced the deck hand-in-hand, whispering sugar-coated delusions about mango groves and golden fortunes, completely oblivious to the chorus of retching around them. A good third of the ship had succumbed to seasickness and lined the rails in a loose brotherhood, I dubbed, *The Fellowship of the Puke*. They stood like mourners at a watery wake, eyes glazed, stomachs mutinous, heaving their hopes and breakfast into the Atlantic with operatic flair.

One particularly committed chap from behind the mountains near the Spanish border, clutching a thermos of ginger ale as if it were holy water. "This is the cure," he whispered with the intensity of a zealot, just moments before doubling over and projectile-confessing to the sea gods. If Poseidon existed, he was getting full service that voyage.

My father, ever the eternal optimist and part-time motivational speaker, treated the deck like his personal TED Talk stage minus the audience and plus a whole lot of nausea. "Africa!" he bellowed, arms flung wide like a televangelist mid-revival. "The land of dreams! The cradle of opportunity!" His voice rang out across the deck, echoing off lifeboats that looked distinctly unconvinced, as if they'd quietly discussed abandoning ship on principle.

He spun tales with the flourish of a mythmaker and the subtlety of a brass band. Dysentery? A chance to build resilience. Sunstroke? A spiritual awakening in vitamin D form. Mosquitoes? Nature's tiny life coaches with wings. His eyes sparkled with a messianic fervour as he surveyed the ship's passengers, clearly mistaking their expressions of seasick despair for rapture.

Meanwhile, my mother had retreated into a private corner of shade where she'd established what I can only describe as a literary refugee camp. Surrounded by warped paperbacks that had begun to curl like autumn leaves, she sat with the posture of a woman quietly negotiating a truce with the tropics, and every so often, she'd peel a damp page off her forearm and mutter, "At least the sweat is good for the pores," in the tone of someone who'd read *Dante's Inferno* and found it oddly relatable.

They were, in essence, two sides of the same absurd coin: one gilded with hope and delusion, the other lacquered in sarcasm and humidity-induced apathy. And somehow, together, they made this floating circus feel almost like a family trip.

The captain was a wiry relic of salt and sinew, with the permanent squint of a man who'd stared too long into sunrises and engine fires. His face looked carved from driftwood, his expression perpetually hovering somewhere between suspicion and scorn. He wore what might once have been a crisp naval uniform, now downgraded to a wearable oil slick, tattooed with decades of mechanical betrayal and the stubborn ghosts of engine grease.

He wasn't so much a leader as a reluctant war general, waging daily combat against the ship's rebellious anatomy. A growler by nature and a stomper by preference, his day began with verbal warfare against the boiler. "You steamin' iron toad!" he'd bellow from the bowels of the ship. "I ask for *heat*, not philosophy!" The boiler, unmoved, hissed back like an insulted cat.

Every piece of equipment had a nickname, and none of them was kind. The radio? "That whisperin' liar." The winch? "A sulking donkey on its lunch break." The navigation compass? "Drunker than the cook," which was saying something. On particularly tense days, he'd storm the deck, wielding a rust-streaked pipe wrench like a pirate with a vendetta. There was talk of him once threatening to hurl the entire engine overboard "to teach it a lesson in humility."

Passengers, especially first-timers, occasionally mistook his tirades for impending doom. But the crew? They barely looked up. They knew this was the captain's courtship ritual, a salty ballet of curses, threats, and reluctant reconciliation. Beneath all the fury was something tender: a grudging love for that wheezing hulk of bolts and steam. The ship, after all, was the only thing that never lied to him, just protested... loudly.

And then there was Carmen gliding down the promenade arm in arm with a different man each day, like a woman auditioning for the role of 'heartbreaker in chief.' She spent more time tucked away in lifeboat number six than most sailors did on duty. For the longest time, I assumed it was just a quirky hiding spot until my teenage years, when the penny dropped, and I realised that innocent little lifesaving vessel wasn't a refuge. It was the ship's unofficial brothel.

When we finally limped into Maputo, the captain stood tall at the bridge, arms folded, eyes narrowed against the glare. The sun caught the twisted metal of the railings, which glinted like a war medal pinned to a battle-scarred chest. He surveyed the battered vessel, nodded once, and muttered with the weary reverence of a man who'd just survived a long and passionate argument with fate, "Held together with spit and madness... but she made it."

Time at sea stretches like taffy: sticky, slow, and strangely hypnotic. Days folded into each other with the flaccid repetition of a broken record. And if there was one thing more unpredictable than the waves, it was the food.

Meals aboard the ship were less a culinary experience and more a game of dietary roulette. Each dish served by the galley arrived with the same level of fanfare as an unwanted telegram. Breakfast usually consisted of rubbery eggs with the structural integrity of flip-flops and toast that bore a suspicious resemblance to plywood. Coffee, if one could call it that, was a thick, tar-like brew capable of stripping paint. On occasion, we were offered porridge, which slouched in the bowl like a sullen teenager, lumpy, reluctant, and cold in the centre.

Lunch was no reprieve. The cook, a man with a body shaped like a barrel and an apron that looked like it had fought in three wars, had an irrational devotion to grey meats. Everything was either over-boiled or under-spiced, or both. Meatloaf made its appearance so frequently that we suspected it was breeding in the pantry. The stew was the real star, a mysterious concoction that jiggled with an unsettling enthusiasm. Peas floated like survivors on a lifeboat, and the potatoes had the texture of despair. And through it all, the cook remained cheerfully unfazed by the chaos because he was always, without exception, completely and gloriously drunk.

Yes, the reason the cook never once got seasick wasn't some supernatural gift or hardened stomach from years at sea. No, it was gin, rum, or Brandy. Whatever was closest to hand and strongest in scent. His breath could sterilise a scalpel. He cooked with a bottle in one hand and a song in his lungs, staggering around the galley like a sailor on shore leave. The only thing steadier than his hands was his devotion to nutmeg.

Dinners tried their best to be fancy. The tablecloths were laid, the chairs straightened, and the soup bowls filled with liquid approximations of flavour. We endured tomato bisque that tasted of tinned metal and onion broth that left our eyes watering not from the onions, but from the vague existential sadness it invoked. Desserts were ambitious but ill-fated. One night, we were presented with a pudding so dense it could have been used as ballast. Another time, we were offered custard that had clearly given up during the cooking process and now existed only as a philosophical concept.

The cook, bless his pickled soul, believed in the power of seasoning. Unfortunately, he only ever used nutmeg, and in quantities that bordered on war crimes. He sang while he worked, usually sea shanties repurposed with culinary lyrics: "Oh the gravy was thick as the ocean wide, and the beef was lost in the tide!" We'd hear him bellowing over the sound of ladles slapping pots. Occasionally, he'd fall asleep against a sack of flour mid-song and wake up shouting for more cloves.

Despite everything, he was beloved. There was something comforting about his chaotic presence, a drunken, sweaty guardian of terrible meals. He never wavered, never paused, never vomited. He might forget to add salt or accidentally serve the same dish three nights in a row, but he was ours. And he never let us go hungry.

His most memorable creation was something he referred to only as "The Surprise." It arrived unannounced and unidentifiable. One night, it crunched. The next, it purred. There was a lot of debate over whether it had been alive that morning. But it filled stomachs and distracted minds. And at sea, that was enough.

His most infamous moment came on what would later be dubbed "Curry Catastrophe Night." He'd somehow gotten his hands on a crate of overripe bananas and two dozen tins of expired curry powder. The result was a dish that smelled like tropical despair and tasted like punishment. Passengers wept openly. A few suspected this was his way of getting revenge on those who had questioned his mashed turnips the week before.

The aftermath was truly biblical as people stormed the deck in search of fresh air and forgiveness. Meanwhile, the seasick society, previously loyal to the railings, had migrated en masse to the stern to avoid the aroma. One woman, claiming to be a food psychic, even declared she had seen a vision of the curry attacking us in our sleep. Ultimately, even Edith, who had proudly stomached every dish without complaint, poked her fork into the yellow mush and whispered, "This is where my courage ends."

The cook himself, however, was undeterred. He took a triumphant swig from a tin cup of something probably illegal, slapped a ladle on the counter, and said, "Tell the captain we're ready for dessert." Dessert, as it happened, was rum-soaked prunes served flambé, though the flames may have been accidental, the result of his sleeve catching fire near the stove. The fire was extinguished with a wet apron and a lot of shouting, and dessert was served half-burnt and completely unapologetic.

Despite or perhaps because of his culinary crimes, the cook became a kind of legend. Children avoided the galley, certain that he slept with pickled eggs under his pillow. Adults treated him with wary affection, offering polite nods and whispered prayers before meals. And yet, when he passed through the dining room, drunkenly whistling "My Bonnie Lies Over the Ocean," he was met with applause. Not because we enjoyed his food. But because he showed up. Because he fed us. Because somehow, against all odds, he cared.

His final meal before we docked in Maputo was both underwhelming and unforgettable. A fish pie of questionable heritage, topped with something that might once have been mashed potatoes but had taken on the consistency of spackling paste. As the gangplank lowered and we disembarked, someone raised a toast to him with a chipped mug of coffee. "To the man who kept us fed. Or at least full."

The cook took a bow, burped loudly, and shouted, "Bon appétit!"

And with that, we stepped off the ship into the blinding light of a new world, our stomachs uneasy, our spirits strangely lifted, and our memories forever etched with the taste of nutmeg and bravery.

Maputo, seen from the ship, had shimmered like a mirage; now, standing on its dock, it felt like being swallowed whole by the sun. The air wrapped itself around us like a damp wool coat soaked in spice, sweat, and diesel. Crates were being unloaded with violent precision, goats darted between the legs of shouting dock workers, and someone had already dropped a suitcase into the harbour.

We stood dazed, a ragtag parade of overfed, underslept passengers blinking like newborns. After thirty days of maritime misery, the earth beneath our feet felt suspiciously solid, too solid. Several passengers dropped to their knees in dramatic displays of gratitude or vertigo.

Edith stood beside me, fanning herself with her deck of playing cards. "I can smell adventure," she said, before immediately clarifying, "No, wait, that's definitely fish."

My mother's hair had expanded to twice its usual volume thanks to the humidity. She was trying to maintain her composure while dragging a suitcase that had lost one wheel and possibly part of its soul. My father, beaming, declared, "This is it! The gateway to opportunity! The continent of promise!"

From somewhere behind us, the cook shouted, "If it's got rum, I'm staying!"

It was not long before confusion reigned supreme, as port officials barked orders in Portuguese, which few of us understood. As a result, luggage went one way and passengers another, while the smell of the dock, equal parts ocean brine and fermented mango, seemed to cling to our very thoughts. Amidst this chaos, I watched as an elderly woman tried to bribe a customs officer with a tin of sardines; he accepted it with a shrug. Furthermore, one child, clearly traumatised by the curry incident, refused to eat anything unless it came in a sealed tin, while Edith stole a mango from a vendor and justified it with, "Consider it emotional compensation."

Despite the chaos, something else stirred, something like hope. Even as we wiped the sweat from our brows and grumbled about missing trunks, there was an unmistakable flicker of curiosity in our eyes. The voyage had battered us, yes. But it had also, somehow, bound us.

And as we marched, staggered, really off the docks and into the blistering unknown, I realised the journey wasn't ending.

This was only the beginning.

Chapter 6:
Mornings at the Madhouse.

Moving to another country felt like stepping into a storm with no map and no shelter. At barely nine years old, the uncertainty of it all wreaked havoc on me, which is why I struggled to concentrate and floundered in school. I slowly shrank into myself, becoming shy and withdrawn, and began disconnecting from both my family and my classmates.

Academically, I was drowning. No matter how hard I tried, the words on the page blurred, the numbers tangled, and my brain simply refused to cooperate. It wasn't long before my learning difficulties became a running joke in the family, something to be laughed at rather than understood.

Support? Non-existent.

Every mistake, failed test, and stammered answer only seemed to confirm what everyone already believed: that I was slow, different, not quite enough. And when you're a child, you don't fight those labels. You absorb and believe them.

As I huddled on the frosty concrete floor, my head tucked between my knees like an ostrich failing miserably at camouflage, my father's voice boomed through the mansion's corridors. It was a blistering Friday afternoon, the kind where you could fry an egg on the sidewalk or, in our case, cook up a full-blown family drama without the need for a stove.

"He's about as sharp as a marble, lazy as a decorating sloth, and has a profound allergy to anything resembling study!"

His words ricocheted off the walls like a misguided missile, each syllable finding its target with unerring precision.

Meanwhile, my uncles and cousins moonlighting as a makeshift brigade of peace negotiators hovered nearby, tossing comforting words around like confetti at a parade that had spectacularly lost its way, but I knew how this production ended.

There I sat, the main character in what was shaping up to be a critically unacclaimed performance titled *"The Belt Chronicles,"* starring my father in his trademark role: the enthusiastic yet directionally challenged disciplinarian.

His leather belt, a notorious escape artist with a flair for improvisation, often flubbed its lines, opting for jazz-style solos on my legs and back. On particularly avant-garde evenings, it might even deliver a command performance against the unsuspecting plaster wall.

And the pièce de resistance? A V-shaped crimson accolade emblazoned across my chest, a not-so-gentle reminder of my unwilling forays into the world of domestic performance art.

At the ripe age of nine, having barely dipped a toe into the murky waters of education, I was already a reluctant aficionado of a genre I'd lovingly dubbed *"Corporal Punishment: Unplugged."*

Each episode left me pondering the critics' reviews, secretly hoping for a sudden series cancellation or at least a plot twist that involved less improvisation with the belt.

Our home, a stronghold of Roman Catholic austerity, worked with the efficiency of a beehive on lockdown. At the heart of this well-oiled machine was my grandmother, a formidable figure cloaked in perpetual black, commanding the troops like a general in skirts. Nothing in the household happened without her stamp of approval, making her the unofficial gatekeeper of our daily lives.

The grand colonial mansion wore its corrugated iron tiara with the weary grace of an aging beauty queen. Its veranda flirted dangerously with splinters, almost as if daring guests to test their luck.

Within its walls, three over-the-top families performed their daily melodrama, each more committed to the spectacle than the last.

And then there was Uncle. A phantom with perfect timing, who shared no blood ties with us unless, of course, spilling red wine on our carpet counted as a familial bond.

He moved through our lives like a ghost who had taken etiquette lessons, always immaculately dressed, as if he were a professor moonlighting as a magician. His coat pockets may well have concealed a deck of cards, a flask of brandy, or the lost secrets of the universe; one could never be sure.

A veritable geyser of knowledge, Uncle spewed facts, theories, and unsolicited wisdom with the gusto of a carnival barker. His expertise ranged from politics to poultices, from Shakespeare to stock markets, always delivered in a tone that suggested we should be taking notes.

Strategically perched at his self-designated seat at the dinner table, he held court like a man who could disappear at any moment, and often did. For instance, one second he was there, mid-sentence about the economy of Zanzibar; however, the next moment brought only a puff of metaphorical smoke and an empty chair.

Mealtimes, in his presence, were part magic show, part TED Talk, and for a brief, glorious moment, he almost made us forget we were eating grandma's experimental casserole again.

As I drifted further from the familial fold, Uncle became my unlikely beacon of hope, a lighthouse in a storm of indifference.

In a family where I was affectionately (or perhaps less-than-affectionately) dubbed "the village idiot," Uncle's bottomless well of knowledge felt like a treasure trove just waiting to be plundered.

I craved warmth, some semblance of affection, but my existential pleas for a simple hug or a word of encouragement were usually met with the enthusiasm of a cat being offered a bath, which is to say, mild horror and a rapid exit.

And so, I retreated into my shell, a self-imposed exile, dreaming of the day when I could return triumphant, dazzling my family with wit and wisdom, ideally, of course, without actually opening my mouth and ruining the effect.

Schooling for me was akin to trying to catch water with a sieve, an endeavour both futile and damp. Punishment for academic missteps became as routine as breakfast, only less nourishing and more painful.

While my peers and buddies were off gallivanting on golden sands, they engaged in the high-stakes world of competitive sandcastle construction. They slathered themselves with enough sunscreen to slide off their beach chairs; meanwhile, I found myself enlisted in the considerably less glamorous Dad's Construction Co. Summer Camp for the Tan-Challenged. Here, the preferred beach accessory was a hard hat, and the closest thing to a wave was the occasional heat haze that shimmered over hot concrete.

Amidst the symphony of clangs and the vibrant lexicon of "creative" worker expressions (which I'm pretty sure weren't included in my school textbooks), I stumbled upon an oasis of sorts. Picture a world where blending into the background as the sun takes its curtain call is just part of the gig. Imagine a musical ensemble of iron and exuberance, serving up a daily platter of benign neglect, dished out by a crew so engrossed in their ballet of brawn and sweat that one lesser-spotted apprentice going AWOL barely made the bulletin.

This wasn't your average summer getaway; it was more of an accidental adventure in invisibility and impromptu endurance training, peppered with the kind of life lessons you definitely can't get from building a sandcastle, like how to dodge a flying hammer with the grace of a matador or interpret the nuanced dialect of construction site banter. And so, as my friends tanned and frolicked in the surf, I honed my skills in the art of unnoticed contributions to the urban landscape, all the while cultivating a complexion that could best be described as "Eau de Concrete."

My journey home each evening, under a canopy of stars, turned into an epic trek rivalling the voyages of ancient heroes, leading up to the night's main event. This wasn't your average TV drama; this was a live critique of my timekeeping skills, delivered with the zest and zeal of a Michelin-starred chef unveiling his latest culinary masterpiece. It was, in its own twisted way, the perfect capstone to each day's adventures in the world of bricks and mortar.

Yet, in this world where child labour was as standard as breakfast cereal, my imagination soared beyond the mortar and bricks. I dreamt of flipping the script, envisioning a future where those very workers, along with my father, would be on my payroll, dancing to the tune I called. This vision, a sweet concoction of ambition and youthful defiance, eventually crystallised into reality, decades later. The twist? My father wasn't part of the ensemble cast in this production, but the stage was set, and the dream was alive and kicking.

***

Meanwhile, back at the colonial mansion, at the stroke of 10:00 AM sharp as reliably as a comedian's punchline, the local culinary maestro made his grand entrance through the rear hall.

Picture this: a scene straight out of a Food Network fever dream, featuring a wicker basket so enormous it could double as a small canoe, festooned with African beads so vibrant they could make a rainbow self-conscious.

This basket, however, wasn't just a container. It was a cornucopia of possibilities, a treasure chest of culinary potential, brimming with the freshest bounties of the land.

Enter the Matriarch.

Standing at the helm of this gastronomic kingdom was my grandmother, the iron-fisted sovereign of the kitchen, a woman whose standards made Michelin inspectors look like amateurs.

She conducted her daily inspection with the precision of a drill sergeant at a military parade, her razor-sharp gaze slicing through produce with the same efficiency she wielded over her domain.

Vegetables that dared show up with the flaccid audacity of a limp handshake? Dismissed on sight. Meats with a little too much indulgent marbling? Given the cold shoulder faster than a comedian bombing on stage.

And fish? Oh, those poor, unfortunate fish, if their eyes were cloudier than a British summer, they were banished without appeal, ushered out with a swiftness that would make an uninvited salesman jealous.

But this wasn't just a selection process; this was a culinary casting call, where only the freshest, crispest, and most vibrant ingredients survived.

Anything that dared fall short wasn't just rejected, it was subjected to one of Grandma's legendary critiques.

And trust me, even the bravest of carrots trembled at the thought.

Dinner was a tightly orchestrated affair, each child seated like a duck in a row, our initials engraved on mahogany rings, as if we were tagged specimens in a very peculiar zoo, well-fed, well-groomed, but unmistakably on display.

On one side of the table, the adults' realm was a glittering showcase of opulence, silverware polished to a mirror shine, porcelain so delicate it looked as though it might shatter if we so much as breathed near it. Meanwhile, on our side? The humble, functional wares of childhood survival, plates that bore the scars of many a questionable meal and ill-fated tantrum.

Yet, no matter the setting, the meals themselves were nothing short of theatrical. Beasts and fish, roasted, boiled, and baked into submission, were paraded before us in a spectacle so elaborate it bordered on ritualistic.

Some dishes seemed to stare back, their lifeless eyes locked in a silent, existential plea, as if to question their role in this strange, gilded tableau.

In this circus of a household, comedy and tragedy were dance partners locked in an endless, uneasy tango, their steps intertwined, indistinguishable.

More often than not, I was cast as the reluctant clown, slipping on the metaphorical banana peel of life while the world laughed, winced, or simply carried on with dinner.

Yet, in the midst of chaos and belt lashes, somewhere between the roars of laughter and the echoes of discipline, lay the foundation of tales too absurd to be anything but fondly remembered.

Just as dinner was a punctual affair at 7:30 PM sharp, lights out for us kids followed at 9:30 PM, without fail, a strictly enforced rule, as predictable as the sun setting or Grandma disapproving of something. But the night? The night was merely an intermission.

As we nestled into our beds, swallowed by the tomb-like silence of our communal dormitory, the thin walls, flimsy as the plot of a bad soap opera, became the unintended conduit for our nightly entertainment.

The evening's auditory lineup was nothing if not eclectic.

The passionate symphony of my parents' love-making sessions acted as a bold opening act, performed with the unapologetic enthusiasm of a live audience as if they had forgotten the walls weren't actually soundproof. Seamlessly layered beneath this, Grandma's murmured rosary prayers began. Each bead slid through her fingers like she was trying to bargain with heaven against the unholy debauchery taking place down the hall.

And just when we thought the show couldn't possibly get more avant-garde, came Uncle's signature performance, a crescendo of thunderous farts, each one punctuating his grand exit from the house like a man composing his own bass-heavy requiem.

Step. Fart. Step. Fart. Step. Finale.

It was a nightly farce, a carefully orchestrated chaos, and we, the hidden audience, attended with the eagerness of theatregoers at a sold-out show.

Every night, without fail, we lay in the dark, stifling giggles, eyes wide in amazement, marvelling at the accidental symphony life under our roof had to offer.

Every morning in our household played out like the opening scene of a slapstick comedy about the world's most chaotic relay race. The alarm clock was our starting gun. From the moment it shrieked to life, the house exploded into a frenzy that would make Olympic sprinters rethink their training regimens.

First came the bed exodus, an uncoordinated stampede of half-awake bodies tripping over blankets and each other in an attempt to be first to the bathroom. This hallway was a battleground of yawning warriors that saw swift alliances and betrayals, especially as bathroom access was a prize won only by cunning or sheer luck.

Those too slow to claim a sink found themselves brushing their teeth in doorways or perched on the edge of bathtubs. In particularly desperate moments, some were even reduced to using the kitchen tap while dodging breakfast preparations.

Laundry piles served as treacherous terrain, clothes from the previous day strewn like casualties of an unseen battle. Socks, elusive as ever, seemed to vanish into the abyss overnight, leading to frantic searches and inevitable mismatches. Combs and hairbrushes were communal resources, passed from hand to hand in an intricate barter system, and anyone lucky enough to tame their bedhead before leaving the house was considered something of a minor deity.

The entire spectacle led up to the final act breakfast at exactly 7:00 AM. There was no flexibility in the schedule, no room for tardiness. Our grandmother, the household's chief enforcer of order, ensured that breakfast was served with the precision of a military operation. The clatter of dishes signalled the transition from chaos to discipline, as everyone assumed their assigned seats, a formation as unyielding as the rest of the morning routine.

Uncle, as always, arrived early, his stomach growling its own morning greeting, an ominous prelude to his two-part performance. The first act involved inhaling food at an alarming speed, his fork and knife moving with the precision of a seasoned duellist. The second act was even more dramatic: his latest batch of news, dispensed with the confidence of a prime-time anchor delivering breaking headlines.

The adults' side of the table was a bastion of refined excess. Plates adorned with leftovers from the previous night's feast, grilled meats, cheeses, and dense breads formed an intimidating spread. Among them, a particularly unsettling sight made its usual appearance: the eyeless fish. Uncle, with the enthusiasm of an eccentric scientist, had plucked out their eyes the night before, a tradition that seemed to serve no purpose other than his own satisfaction. Now, the fish lay there in their porcelain tombs, their lifeless bodies arranged in a way that suggested they still had some regrets about their life choices.

Breakfast for us kids felt less like a meal and more like an ongoing experiment in human endurance, curated by a mad scientist with a flair for culinary chaos. The main act was a dish so bewildering it could only have been conceived during a game of culinary roulette, pork brains, and scrambled eggs, swimming in a condensed milk reduction. It was a meal that defied logic, taste buds, and basic human decency, the kind of concoction that left us all questioning our place in the universe before the school day had even begun.

And then, as if that weren't punishment enough, came the grand finale, a generous drizzle of cod-liver oil, the cherry on top of our morning torture cake. This breakfast wasn't just about nutrition; it was a test of willpower, a daily psychological battle that made Uncle's bizarre, but increasingly appetising, eyeless fish banquet seem like a gourmet escape.

By the time the clock threatened to strike 8:00, our front door transformed into the starting line of a high-stakes family Olympics, each of us poised to launch ourselves into the world as if escaping from captivity. Parents, siblings, and cousins lined up with the intensity of athletes, eyes fixed on the ultimate prize, temporary freedom from the regimented joys of home life. The atmosphere was electric, crackling with the desperate energy of a group determined to flee before another round of domestic duties caught them in its grip.

Meanwhile, standing in the cavernous space of our near-empty home, left behind like the last survivor in an epic saga, was Uncle, our household's very own Marco Polo of the airwaves, an explorer of radio frequencies rather than foreign lands.

While the rest of us scrambled out the door, he remained behind, armed with nothing but his sharp wit and his beloved radio, a technological relic so grandiose it could have doubled as a vintage automobile in disguise.

This wasn't just any radio. No, this was the Bakelite beast, the wooden wonder of the airwaves, a gargantuan contraption that ruled the living room with all the pomp and self-importance of an eccentric sovereign lounging on his throne.

It hissed and crackled like a restless oracle, offering news, weather, and the occasional static-laced mystery, all while Uncle presided over it like a high priest deciphering the sacred signals of the world beyond our walls.

With his legs crossed and coffee in hand, he basked in the ritual of his morning broadcasts. He was content in the knowledge that while the rest of us faced the trials of school and work, he would spend his day in the company of voices drifting in from distant lands. He remained perfectly at home in his kingdom of static and stories.

With a casual twist of the dial, Uncle morphed into a world-class explorer, minus the actual travel. He could be sipping tea in the heart of Africa one minute and dodging taxis in downtown America the next, all with the nonchalance of a seasoned globetrotter. This mammoth machine was more than a mere appliance; it was the centrepiece of our living room and Uncle's ticket to daily auditory adventures.

This behemoth of the bandwidth didn't just fill a corner; it dominated the room, demanding homage from all who dared enter. There, enthroned amidst upholstery and throw pillows, Uncle charted his course through distant lands and exotic locales, proving that all you really need for a bit of globe-trotting is a hefty radio, a vivid imagination, and maybe a little too much time on your hands.

This monstrous machine wasn't merely an object in the room. It was a conversation starter, a storyteller, and a magnet for intrigue and speculation. Its presence in the corner of the colonial house's living room made it a focal point, a piece of family lore that provoked endless discussions and debates. It was the guardian of the globe's secrets, sitting quietly in our living room. Meanwhile, Uncle, the lone audience member, embarked on his daily voyages from the comfort of his armchair. He proved that you don't need to leave home to have an adventure, especially if you have a radio that's seen more of the world than most of us ever will.

And just when you thought the morning madness had reached its finale, the sequel, "Lunch: The Reckoning," premiered promptly at 1:00 PM. Here we had a culinary dichotomy: a minimalist, almost zen-like offering for the kiddos, and for the adults, a feast that would make a Roman emperor blush, showcasing the morning's victors from the produce parade.

But the true spectacle began post-lunch, marking the onset of the much-dreaded, absolutely mandatory "siesta showdown." This wasn't your picturesque postcard moment of peaceful napping under the sun. Nope, it was more like a silent retreat for the underage crowd, stealthily sneaking off to the dormitory, while the adults embarked on a snoring symphony so robust it could register on the Richter scale. The house transformed into a concert hall, featuring solo performances from various family members, each a testament to the lunch that preceded it. It was a cacophony of z's, a lullaby for none, ensuring that adventure in our household was just a nap away or, more accurately, the lack thereof.

Chapter 7:
Exiled to Derre, the Village that Time Forgot.

The sweltering heat of Zambezi province in Mozambique had a reputation as legendary as its wildlife, which, if it wasn't actively plotting your demise, was at the very least considering it over a long lunch.

The locals had a saying: "If it moves, it kills."

Frankly, this wasn't so much a warning as it was a reminder of the natural order of things. Here, even the mosquitoes had ambition, their tiny, relentless wings humming like a death march in mosquito minor. The humidity was so thick it could have been bottled and sold as soup, and the sun, which loomed overhead like an overzealous interrogator, showed no mercy. And in the heart of this inhospitable stretch of Earth sat Derre, a village so small that if you blinked, you'd miss it, and even if you didn't, you might wish you had.

Time didn't just stand still here; it occasionally took a nap, rolled over, and forgot to set an alarm. Derre wasn't so much a village as it was a geographical afterthought, a place where the roads, if you could call them that, were more philosophical concepts than actual infrastructure. Directions were given in relation to trees, termite mounds, and the occasional abandoned truck that had been swallowed by the landscape.

Electricity existed in theory but was about as reliable as a politician's promise, flickering in and out like it had somewhere better to be. Running water? That depended on whether the pipes felt cooperative that day. And communication with the outside world relied on one man, a bicycle, and a vague sense of urgency.

The people of Derre, however, were nothing if not resilient. Life here had hardened them into a breed of humans who laughed in the face of discomfort, mostly because complaining took up too much energy. They worked in the heat without so much as a sigh, their bodies accustomed to the relentless furnace of the African sun in a way that defied logic and basic human tolerance.

Hospitality was both a survival tactic and a competitive sport. Visitors, few as they were, were received with a warmth so genuine it could melt steel. Refusing an offering of food or drink wasn't just frowned upon; it was social treason. And the food, oh, the food. It was rich, flavourful, and occasionally unidentifiable, often accompanied by a side of cryptic reassurance:

"Don't worry, it's fresh."

Fresh, *what*, exactly, was a question best left unasked.

Despite the occasional existential crisis that came with every meal, Derre had its own peculiar charm. The night sky, untouched by artificial light, unfolded like a velvet curtain dusted with stars, so crisp and infinite it made you forget, if only briefly, that you were living in a place where nature had the upper hand.

But Derre's greatest feature wasn't the landscape, or the people, or even the bizarre sense of time. It was the stories.

Because in a place where time dripped like molasses and survival often depended on wit as much as resilience, stories were the lifeblood of the village. Tales of battles with oversized insects, legendary fishing escapades, and encounters with spirits who may or may not have been local drunks in disguise were passed around like currency. And here, in this forgotten little corner of the world, everyone had a story to tell.

So, there I was, years ago, banished to Derre like some tragic hero in an epic where the main villain was my own embarrassing academic record. Turns out, being "stupid with learning difficulties," as my father so delicately put it, makes for an excellent excuse to ship your son off to the ends of the Earth.

And Derre? It *was* the end of the Earth plus an extra five miles, just to be sure.

This village had the odd distinction of having everything and nothing, all at once.

Need a hand-cranked flashlight from the 1960s? Check. A pair of underwear that had clearly survived several apocalyptic scenarios? Absolutely. A hammer made from what suspiciously looked like a repurposed aeroplane part? Right over there, next to the canned goods from another century.

The general store was like a museum curated by a drunk time traveller, its dusty shelves an archaeological dig of misplaced decades.

"Organisation" was more of a legend, whispered about but never actually practised. You could find anything here except, of course, something you actually needed.

Take soap, for example. Yes, they had soap. But soap that didn't double as sandpaper? Now that was too much to ask.

The store's gatekeeper, Mr Gomes, was a man whose personality was as dusty and eclectic as his shelves. He took pride in being unpredictable, a quality that extended to his inventory, where expired was simply another word for "aged to perfection." He had the kind of face that suggested he'd witnessed history firsthand, possibly while selling canned sardines during it.

One afternoon, I combed through the chaos of rusted tins and soap brands that had long since vanished from the modern world. It was then that Mr Gomes emerged from behind the counter, appearing like a magician unveiling his final trick. In his hand, he held a bar of chocolate so old it looked like it had been hand-delivered by Vasco da Gama himself.

"Can I interest you in a vintage treat?" he asked, holding it out with the reverence of a sacred relic. The wrapper was faded, brittle, and bore the logo of a brand I was fairly certain had gone out of business during the last century.

I stared at it, imagining it had seen multiple economic collapses and at least one border skirmish. It looked more like a fossil than a snack.

"Still sealed," Mr Gomes noted helpfully. "Might be dusty, but the spirit of cocoa lives on."

"I prefer my chocolate without a side of colonial nostalgia," I said, giving him a look that suggested I wouldn't risk my dental future for nostalgia.

He shrugged, undeterred. "Suit yourself. But when civilisation collapses, this will be the closest thing we've got to currency."

And just like that, I realised that Derre's version of survival wasn't just about food, water, and shelter. It was about knowing when to accept the unhinged logic of its inhabitants.

There was a certain irony to life in Derre. It was a place where time forgot to tick, but somehow, every clock was five minutes fast. Where you couldn't buy a can opener, but you could get a Gramophone and the Mozart Requiem in D Minor 12-inch record, practically a survival guide around here. And if you were lucky, you'd make it out alive before you developed an inexplicable attachment to its absurdity.

However, the village did have a charm, one that sneaked up on you like the stray chickens that freely roamed the dirt streets. Much like the weather, the pace of life was relentless and yet slow, and days blurred into each other in a way that made you wonder if the sun was playing a practical joke.

The rural clinic was a masterpiece of minimalist absurdity, half waiting room, half existential test. It was staffed by Nurse Mabel, a woman whose face bore the permanent expression of someone midway through a decades-long sigh. She had perfected the art of appearing as though she'd just finished running a marathon while blindfolded, barefoot, and juggling flaming torches. Her white uniform, perpetually crumpled, gave the impression it had survived both war zones and wash cycles.

Healthcare, in this forgotten outpost, was less a structured service and more a hopeful gesture toward wellness. Remedies ranged from mysterious herbal teas that smelled faintly of burnt grass and resignation, to handwritten prescriptions that looked like grocery lists from another century. On particularly trying days, patients were sent home with a bandage, a boiled sweet, and a weary glance that seemed to say, "Try not dying until Wednesday, I'm off on Thursday."

My first encounter with Nurse Mabel took place on a blistering Thursday afternoon, the kind of day when the sun felt personal, and even the flies looked for shade. I arrived at the clinic clutching my left hand, blood slowly seeping through the handkerchief I'd hastily wrapped around a deep cut on my finger, courtesy of a rusty nail and a poorly judged shortcut through the fence behind the Governor's colonial mansion.

The clinic's waiting area, if one could call two plastic chairs and a drooping ficus a waiting area, was empty, save for a hand-painted sign that read "Patience Heals Faster." I wasn't sure if it was a philosophical statement or a passive-aggressive reminder.

After a few minutes, Nurse Mabel emerged from the back room carrying a tray of what looked like homemade ointments, gauze, and thinly disguised resentment. Her expression was carved from stone and shaded with fatigue.

"Well," she said, eyeing me with the flat stare of someone who had seen far worse and hadn't been impressed then either. "What've we got?"

I held up my hand. "Cut. Nail. Fence."

Mabel nodded and gestured for me to sit on the edge of the examination table, which creaked in protest as if reluctant to participate.

She examined the wound with a grunt, then disappeared into the storeroom, returning with a bottle of something that smelled like equal parts regret and industrial cleaner. "This'll sting," she said, in the tone of someone delivering a prophecy.

It did. I winced hard enough to startle a gecko on the wall.

"That's the infection fleeing your body," she said dryly. "Or your spirit trying to escape. Either way, hold still."

She bandaged the finger with brisk efficiency, wrapping it tighter than necessary. "There," she said, as if completing a minor household chore. "Try not to bleed on anything important for the next few days."

"Do I need a tetanus shot?" I asked.

She paused. "You up for one?"

"I guess?"

She shrugged. "Next shipment's due in a month. Until then, stay away from rust and bad luck."

As I stepped down from the table, flexing my newly mummified finger, Nurse Mabel patted me once on the shoulder.

"You'll live. Most people do. Eventually."

And with that, she vanished behind the curtain again, leaving behind only the faint scent of antiseptic and unspoken advice.

I exited the clinic with a throbbing hand, a clearer understanding of rural healthcare and a reluctant admiration for the iron-willed woman who kept the place running on grit, gauze, and gallows humour.

The bottle store stood as a modest beacon of simplicity, a small temple to intoxicated hope, rising proudly in a sea of dust and confusion. It boasted an exclusive selection of only two beverages, as relayed to me by a lanky young recluse peering out from behind the iron bars of the local jail. First, there was the beer, thick, warm, and suspiciously reminiscent of liquid bread, likely the outcome of a brewer with more ambition than talent. Then came the red wine, so tart and sun-scorned it made you question whether someone had accidentally left the grapes out too long, sour regret in a bottle. Ultimately, choosing between the two was less a matter of taste and more a test of one's adventurous spirit, or perhaps just a thirst desperate enough to lower expectations and raise eyebrows.

In Derre, the charm lived in its contradictions. You could stroll into the general store and emerge with everything you never knew you didn't need, limp into the clinic and receive a bandage so indifferent it might've come with an apology, and pop into the bottle store for a cold drink only to leave wondering if thirst was the wiser choice. It was a village that thrived on quirky scarcity, a place where daily survival felt like a low-budget comedy, full of missed cues, strange treasures, and the occasional miracle in a tin can.

And then there was the Thursday night reunion, a weekly gathering that could only be described as the closest thing to a gentleman's club that Derre could muster. Around an improvised poker table, really just an old door propped up on rickety crates, sat the Governor, the general store owner, the bottle store owner, and the priest, each wearing expressions that ranged from casual indifference to intense concentration. It was the kind of motley crew that made you wonder what secrets and scandals were being shuffled along with the cards.

A young servant, whose primary job seemed to be ensuring that no glass ever went dry, moved silently around the table, topping up the whiskey in locally made terracotta glasses that had all the elegance of clay mugs but none of the refinement. The men sipped their drinks with the nonchalance of those who had long since abandoned the idea that anything stronger than water might actually taste good. They snacked on peanuts and dried cod fish, which, to the uninitiated, might seem like a punishment rather than a treat. But here, it was all part of the rustic charm.

Meanwhile, I, along with the Governor's little bugger, entertained ourselves nearby, completely oblivious to the high-stakes game unfolding just a few feet away. We played with handmade cars, which were lovingly crafted by appreciative tribe members out of bits of wood and scrap metal. These were no ordinary toys; rather, they were prized possessions, the kind of gifts that had more heart and soul in them than anything you'd find in a city shop. Furthermore, our makeshift racetrack was the dirt floor, and our races were as intense as the poker game, even though our winnings were more likely to be bragging rights than any tangible reward.

The air was thick with the smell of whiskey, sweat, and the faint aroma of dried fish, a combination that, while far from pleasant, was somehow comforting in its familiarity. The laughter and banter at the poker table provided a soundtrack to our play, punctuated by the occasional groan of frustration or whoop of victory. It was a night of simple pleasures and even simpler wagers, where the line between camaraderie and competition blurred in the haze of alcohol and smoke.

In Derre, Thursday nights were less about winning and more about the ritual. It was a gathering of men who, despite their differences, found common ground in a game of cards and the bottom of a whiskey glass. For us kids, it was a chance to be part of something bigger, even if we didn't fully understand it yet. We were the silent witnesses to the night's antics, learning more about life from the poker table than any classroom could ever teach us.

But towering above it all was the Governor's mansion, a massive colonial relic perched on a hill, overlooking the village like an indifferent deity. The mansion was to Derre what the Playboy Mansion was to Beverly Hills, provided that Hugh Hefner had a fondness for bushveld and questionable morals. Behind those gleaming white walls, anything went. The booze flowed freely, the parties were wild, and no one blinked twice at the tangled heap of lovers, locals, and imported decadence.

For reasons that remain as elusive as the motives behind my youthful escapades, school holidays occasionally found me in this remote outpost. My companion was a school friend whose father, the Governor, ruled over the district with the kind of casual authority that comes with an excess of gin and a shortage of real problems. However, their names escape me now, lost in the haze of those sun-bleached memories.

The journey from the main city to Derre was an adventure in itself, a day-long ordeal in a State-provided Land-Rover that had seen better days and smoother roads. We'd set off at dawn, hoping to reach the village by early afternoon, though this was optimistic at best. The jungle had its own agenda, and it often involved extended delays as we waited for a herd of elephants to lazily saunter across our path or a Mozambique Spitting Cobra to demonstrate its impressive range.

Upon arrival, we were greeted by a small army of servants, all clad in immaculate khaki uniforms with polished buttons and Fez hats that seemed as out of place as we did. They whisked us inside, where a lavish meal awaited, though we were too caked in dust and too disoriented by the heat to fully appreciate it.

The British colonial influence was everywhere, like an unwelcome guest who had overstayed their welcome but still expected to be served tea. The Governor's household operated on the same principles: a strict servant-master hierarchy and a constant stream of soldiers passing through, exchanging favours for a hot meal, a bed for the night, or whatever else the Governor decided they deserved.

One of the most eagerly anticipated events in the otherwise sleepy village of Derre was the monthly safari party, a weekend of debauchery that lured the city's elite like moths to a flame or, perhaps more accurately, like thirsty hippos to a dwindling watering hole. It was a spectacle of excess that made even the most seasoned revellers raise an eyebrow, and it was exactly the kind of thing that kept the Governor in a perpetual good mood or at least a perpetual gin-induced haze.

The arrival of the city folk was an event in itself. They came in droves, their fancy cars kicking up clouds of dust that would linger in the air like the smell of overripe fruit. By the time they stepped out, they were covered in a fine layer of Zambezi grit, giving them the appearance of slightly dishevelled explorers rather than the pampered elite they were. But nothing a good gin and tonic couldn't fix, right? And there was gin aplenty. Sundowners on Friday were practically a law you dared not break unless you fancied being the subject of endless gossip.

The Governor, ever the gracious host, made sure everyone's glass was filled to the brim and that no one noticed the rather alarming rate at which the gin stock was depleting. As the sun dipped below the horizon, casting a warm glow over the savannah, the banquet began. And what a feast it was! The table groaned under the weight of roasted game, exotic fruits, and enough side dishes to feed a small army or at least a very hungry battalion of soldiers who might drop by for scraps later.

If the food didn't knock you out, the conversation might. By this time, the alcohol had begun to work its magic, loosening tongues and inhibitions alike. There were whispers of business deals that would never materialise, scandalous affairs that everyone already knew about, and outrageous bets placed on the next day's safari. Would Mr Thompson, the portly banker, finally bag a leopard? Or would he, as usual, end up face-first in a bush, snoring away last night's indiscretions?

Saturday morning was the real test, though "morning" was perhaps a generous term. By the time anyone was ready to even think about hunting, it was well past dawn. Bleary-eyed and still dressed in the remnants of their evening attire, the guests would stumble into the Land Rovers with rifles in hand, though these were more like props than tools of the trade. The Governor, ever the optimist, would lead the charge; his enthusiasm remained undimmed by the fact that half his party looked as if they'd been dragged through the bush backward, which, to be fair, some of them might have been.

The plan was always the same: a dawn departure to a shallow lake where the local wildlife gathered for their morning drink. The prize of the hunt was a leopard, its skin destined to become a coat that would be utterly impractical in Africa, but the talk of the town back in the motherland. The Governor's veranda was already adorned with over twenty such skins, each one a testament to the excesses of colonial sport, not to mention the scattered elephant tusks that hinted at a different kind of trophy hunting.

The safari itself was less a hunt and more a comedy of errors. The animals, well-versed in the ways of these monthly invasions, had long since learned to steer clear of the chaos. The occasional impala might dart across the path, more out of curiosity than fear, only to watch with something akin to bemusement as the city folk fumbled with their rifles and missed by a mile. If there was any hunting to be done, it was mostly for shade and water and possibly the nearest bush to retch behind.

As the day wore on and the chances of actually catching anything dwindled, the mood would shift from hopeful determination to resigned amusement. "Well, at least we're out in nature," someone would say, as if that justified the entire farce. And in a way, it did. By the time they returned to the mansion, sweaty, sunburned, and more than a little disappointed, the whole ordeal had taken on a rosy glow of nostalgia. The stories they'd tell that evening would be more about the near-misses and the hilarious mishaps than any serious hunting.

And so, the cycle continued, month after month. The safari party was less about bagging big game and more about the stories that would be told afterwards, the camaraderie forged in shared absurdity, and the understanding that in the Zambezi province, the real prize wasn't the leopard's skin but the laughter shared around the fire at the end of the day.

At the tender age of ten, I was more interested in what happened after dark than in the hunt. From my bedroom window, I would watch the adults gather around a roaring fire, drinking and engaging in activities that I only half understood. The Governor, always the life of the party, often had a young local girl perched on his lap, while others paired off or formed more creative arrangements in the shadows.

And then there was Mrs Cruz, the enigmatic wife of a renowned pathologist who arrived for the safari escapade with her *trusted companion*, a brooding gentleman named Arjun Mehra, originally from Udaipur. Whispers followed them like dust on a gravel road. Arjun, it was said, possessed certain... outsized qualities, both in mystery and reputation. The couple rarely emerged from their suite, leaving the rest of us to speculate whether they had come for the wildlife or simply brought their own.

The next morning, the house reeked of stale sweat and spilled liquor, a potent reminder of the night before. The servants, ever efficient, went about their tasks with practised indifference. One old man, stationed under a sprawling jacaranda tree, meticulously prepared the leopard skins on a thick wooden table. The process was a slow and deliberate one; each skin was soaked in salt water, laid out to dry, and then painstakingly scraped to achieve a softness that belied its origins.

Despite the abundance of servants, the true currency in the Governor's household wasn't power or prestige; it was food. As a gesture of goodwill or perhaps quiet diplomacy, a massive cauldron of porridge, thick with corn or manioc flour, was kept simmering over an open fire from sunrise to dusk. Men, women, and children would gather in dusty circles, scooping generous handfuls onto dented enamel plates, dipping them into tins of fiery tomato, chilli, and onion relish that bit back with every mouthful. It wasn't much, but it filled bellies and softened tempers. And long after the last bite was taken, the scent hung in the air a smoky, spicy ghost of sustenance that blurred the line between survival and something close to comfort in this overlooked corner of the world.

Chapter 8:
Nunes the Governor and Rita the Cow.

The so-called "holiday" in Derre was nothing more than my parents' cleverly disguised scheme to offload me for the summer, spun as an *exciting adventure* with the promise of a new friend. Instead of fun-filled escapades, however, I found myself stranded in a village that felt like a forgotten relic of time. Here, the heat was stifling, the mosquitoes were predatory, and, most importantly, my boredom was relentless.

Meals at the Governor's house were an ongoing experiment in survival, prepared by Maria, a woman with the confidence of a master chef but none of the credentials to back it up. Breakfast could be anything from *oatmeal...ish,* to something that looked vaguely edible but tasted like regret, and questioning it only resulted in being told, *"We keep things rustic."* Meanwhile, the house itself was shared with an entire ecosystem, where bats lived rent-free in the attic, lizards casually strolled across the dinner table, and ants carried out full-scale invasions with military precision. Sleeping became an exercise in vigilance, as every night was a gamble between getting dive-bombed by a bat or discovering some mysterious creature had taken up residence in my bed.

Slowly but surely, my instinct for questioning the bizarre began to fade, replaced by a grudging acceptance of Derre's unspoken rules. I stopped reacting when breakfast felt like an attack on my taste buds, when the ants successfully overran the pantry like a conquering army, and when my companion delivered yet another eerie prediction with a knowing nod, as if he were some kind of mystical village oracle. I learned to haggle like a seasoned street vendor, dodge flying insects with the reflexes of a trained assassin, and most importantly, eat first and ask questions later. Somewhere in the midst of the sun-scorched absurdity, the unidentifiable meals, and the never-ending parade of strange encounters, Derre stopped feeling like a punishment and started feeling like a twisted inside joke that only a few of us were in on.

Speaking of metaphors for suffering, no creature embodied the tragicomedy of my time in Derre more than Rita, the cow. Sweet, overworked Rita. If ever there was an undervalued, underappreciated soul in this village, it was her. She was the backbone of our breakfast table, the true unsung hero, providing an endless supply of milk for an ungrateful crowd who never seemed to acknowledge her sacrifices.

Every morning, without fail, a large jug of fresh milk appeared like magic, except, of course, the magic was just Rita, being milked within an inch of her life.

The consumption levels were staggering. It became less of a drink and more of a competitive sport, as if the entire village had an unspoken agreement to see just how much dairy one could physically ingest before their internal organs rebelled.

"More milk?" someone would inevitably ask, as if we weren't single-handedly responsible for exhausting the poor cow's reserves.

And every time, Rita would stand there, wide-eyed, contemplating the choices that led her to this life of unrelenting servitude.

I could relate.

One morning, as I watched Rita from a distance, her hollow, defeated stare met mine. It was as though she knew, knew we were the reason her once-full udder was now a mere shadow of its former glory. I half-expected her to stage a protest, with tiny placards and a determined march around the barn. "Bovines Unite! No More Milk for You!"

After Rita's daily sacrifice, we'd embark on what was sold as an 'adventure', a trip down to the river for a swim. The river, of course, was populated by creatures that seemed more fitting for a horror movie than a vacation spot. Crocodiles lurked beneath the murky water, and hippos, the true rulers of the riverbanks, patrolled with the same intensity as overzealous nightclub bouncers. And yet, there we were, wading in like we were at a luxurious resort, laughing nervously at the possibility of becoming someone's dinner.

"Think the crocs are full?" someone would joke, and we'd all chuckle, even as our eyes darted around for suspicious ripples in the water. Our police escort, a giant of a man with a fez perched precariously on his head, stood by with his rifle slung over his shoulder. He watched us with a mixture of amusement and boredom, clearly more concerned with looking important than actually keeping us alive. If a crocodile had actually decided to join us for a swim, I doubted he'd do much more than tip his fez in acknowledgement.

After our harrowing brush with crocodile-infested waters, lunch was served, and, as usual, it was a theatrical affair, equal parts absurd and extravagant. The table, dressed in fine linen and mismatched silverware, was a beacon of overkill in a village where the most advanced piece of technology was a hand-cranked radio that probably hadn't seen a tune-up since the First World War.

At the head of the table sat Mr Nunes, the Governor, acting as the self-appointed monarch of this backwater kingdom. He ruled with a glass of imported wine in one hand and an air of casual superiority. To him, we were merely subjects, tolerated, but never quite worthy of his refined company. Furthermore, he swirled his glass with the kind of pretentious flair that suggested he had spent his youth perfecting the art of wine-tasting rather than, say, doing anything remotely useful. Each sip he took was a performance in itself, as though he were considering writing a dissertation on the notes of blackberry and oppression.

Meanwhile, the rest of us were arranged according to some unspoken hierarchy that no one dared question. Adults occupied the prized middle seats, lost enough to the Governor to pretend they were part of the conversation, but far enough to avoid his direct scrutiny. We kids, on the other hand, were unceremoniously exiled to the far end of the table, a no-man's land where our opinions, and our very existence, seemed to be more of an inconvenience than a contribution.

The guest list was a bizarre mix of local characters, each one adding a different flavour to the surreal lunch experience. There was the village undertaker, who, despite his profession, always seemed to have a spring in his step. He laughed with the kind of cheerfulness that made you wonder whether he was secretly enjoying the idea that he'd eventually get all of us in his ledger. Next to him sat the priest, whose enthusiasm for fine wines bordered on scandalous. He approached each bottle with the reverence of a man about to perform a sacred ritual, though his sips were more like gulps, and his blessings more like burps.

It was an odd sight: the man responsible for your last rites clinking glasses with the one who would literally bury you. Between the two of them, it felt like we were having lunch with both ends of life, the one who prepared your soul for the afterlife, and the one who made sure your body got there in style.

Their conversation was, as always, a peculiar blend of morbid humour and philosophical debates. "You know," the undertaker said between bites of roast chicken. "I've always found it fascinating how many people want to be buried in their Sunday best. As if it makes a difference six feet under."

The priest chuckled, swirling his wine glass. "Well, I always say, it's better to be overdressed for the afterlife. You never know who you'll run into."

The two of them laughed like old friends, while the rest of us silently exchanged glances, wondering how this had become our reality. As they refilled their glasses with the same zeal they reserved for their respective callings, I couldn't help but feel like we were witnessing the strangest crossover episode of life and death: 'The Wine Enthusiast meets Six Feet Under.'

The rest of us continued to eat in relative silence, our forks clinking against the plates as we tried not to think too hard about what fresh absurdity would follow lunch.

Afternoons were dedicated to a forced "siesta," a sadistic tradition where we were herded into a stifling bedroom to sweat in silence. Meanwhile, the adults luxuriated in the shade, puffing on cigars and sipping cognac like characters from a noir film. There was no actual resting during siesta, just the slow roasting of our bodies and minds. We spent those hours plotting elaborate escapes, none of which ever succeeded.

The only real joy of the day came in the form of soccer with the village kids, a chaotic mix of barefoot players dressed in rags, or what could only generously be called 'clothes.' The field was less of a field and more of a dust bowl, with patches of stubborn grass clinging to life like it had somehow wandered into the wrong place and decided to stay. The ball, a deflated relic held together by sheer willpower and a few pieces of string, wobbled across the ground as if it, too, had seen better days. But none of that mattered because for that hour, it was pure, unfiltered glory.

Our police escort, who seemed to take on every possible role in the village, guardian, magician, and now, referee, stood on the sidelines with a whistle he rarely used, except when it came to favouring the Governor's son. The boy, a pudgy disaster on the field, couldn't have kicked the ball in a straight line if his life depended on it. But that didn't stop him from being awarded a penalty every time he so much as stumbled, which he did often. "Ref!" we'd shout in unison, our voices rising in a futile protest, knowing full well the game was rigged from the start.

The Governor's son would take his penalty kick, and somehow, despite the ball rolling about as fast as a leisurely stroll, it would be declared a goal. We'd all groan, the village kids rolling their eyes with the kind of practised indifference that only comes from years of knowing you're playing in a game stacked against you. But we kept playing anyway, because despite the obvious favouritism, there was something magical about the dust flying up with every step, the laughter echoing across the makeshift field, and the feeling of being completely free, even in the face of the absurd.

Every sprint, every kick, and every dive into the dirt felt like a small rebellion against the ridiculousness of the day, a reminder that, in this one fleeting moment, nothing mattered but the game. By the end, we were all collapsed in exhaustion, covered in dirt and sweat, but grinning like fools. The Governor's son, of course, would celebrate his "victory" as if he had just won the World Cup, while the rest of us exchanged knowing looks, content in the fact that we had the better victory, the joy of playing, laughing, and losing ourselves in the madness of it all.

By the end of each day, we were a ragtag bunch of sunburned, sweat-soaked, and thoroughly confused individuals. As I lay in bed at night, listening to the rhythmic snoring of the house, I'd replay the day's absurd events in my head, shaking my head at the sheer ridiculousness of it all. Another day in Derre, where cows, crocodiles, and cosmic humour ruled the land.

Chapter 9:
The Bonds that Saved me.

And so, I returned home from the so-called "adventure" that had devolved into a fever dream where hippos were slaughtered to feed the locals, and leopards were skinned to fashion coats for the colonial elite lounging comfortably back in the capital. It wasn't the kind of holiday that left you with fond memories, more like one that gave you a permanent aversion to anything involving safari animals or colonial grandeur.

The journey back to civilisation from the dusty village of Derre was as exhausting as it was bizarre. Wedged into the back of a Land Rover, I was surrounded by a chaotic assortment of rural supplies: crates of clucking chickens and a milk can filled to the brim, Rita's final contribution to my diet of dairy excess. As the vehicle rattled down endless dirt roads under a relentless sun, the chickens eyed me with what I could only describe as suspicion. Ultimately, it was a journey that felt like it might never end, leaving the air heavy with a shared sense of being completely done with it all.

Just when I thought the nightmare of abandonment was over, and I could settle into the relative boredom of home, another surprise ambushed me a few days later.

The clink of silverware against porcelain was the only sound filling the dining room that evening. That was, until my father, never one for unnecessary pleasantries, decided to drop a sentence that would change my life forever.

"We've decided to send you to boarding school," he announced, his tone as casual as if he were commenting on a shift in the weather. No grand preamble, no soft cushion of reassurance, just a cold, hard statement, delivered with the precision of a man ticking off an item on a to-do list.

I froze, fork suspended mid-air, the half-chewed bite of chicken in my mouth suddenly turning to sawdust. "Boarding school?" I echoed, as if saying the words aloud would somehow make them less real.

My father, ever the pragmatic enforcer of discipline, nodded. "You haven't been doing well in school," he continued, as if this were breaking news to me. "Maybe over there, they'll knock some sense into you, and you'll start studying harder."

There it was, blunt, unvarnished, and served up without so much as a side of sympathy. The verdict had been reached, and the sentence was about to be carried out. My fate, it seemed, had been discussed and decided upon without me having a seat at the table.

A quiet sort of panic began to rise in my chest, but I tamped it down before it could reach my face. I wanted to protest, to tell him that learning difficulties weren't something you could punish out of a child, that I wasn't some unruly mutt in need of stricter training. My mind screamed with rebuttals; with words I knew would never find their way past my lips. Because what would be the point?

I was eleven. And eleven is an age where you learn often the hard way that in the great hierarchy of the household, you have about as much power as a stray sock in a washing machine. So, instead of fighting, instead of pleading, I did what I had learned to do so well. I nodded.

A small, almost imperceptible gesture, but inside, something deeper shifted. Maybe, just maybe, this was my way out. A ticket to something different. An escape from a house where I was more of a tolerated presence than a cherished son.

My younger brother, now he was the golden child, the one who soaked up the praise, the attention, the admiration. My parents adored him with the kind of reverence usually reserved for child prodigies, while I was the afterthought, the one who struggled, who fell short, who couldn't quite measure up.

Perhaps boarding school would be a reprieve. A break from the endless comparisons, from the sighs of disappointment, from the silent but suffocating expectation that I should be more like him.

There was something oddly liberating about having no say in what happened next. It was a strange kind of freedom, like drifting in a current, knowing that wherever it took me, at least it wouldn't be here. Maybe this new chapter would be different. Maybe, in the absence of home, I'd finally get the chance to figure out who I was beyond the shadow of someone else's success.

So, I let my fate unfold. Not because I wanted it, but because, for the first time, I understood that sometimes, surrendering is the only control you have.

And in that moment, as I stared at the cold, untouched food on my plate, I realised I wasn't just being sent away.

I was being set free.

And so, preparations were set into motion immediately, as though my "incarceration" couldn't come soon enough. The large trunk that had once served me during family trips, filled with the excitement of vacations and adventure, was now repurposed as my schooling dowry, a wooden coffin of sorts, stuffed with bedding, toiletries, and every essential dictated by the school's strict list. It was less a suitcase and more a symbol of my exile, a physical reminder that I was being sent away, not just to learn, but to endure. Indeed, every moment of this process felt cold and distant, as if I were being prepared for banishment rather than education. As a result, I was packed off with the same efficient detachment one might send a parcel through the post.

The following year, just after Easter, I was driven to Barberton, South Africa, wedged into the stifling back seat of my uncle's old VW Beetle. Indeed, the car's cramped interior seemed a fitting metaphor for my life at that moment: confined, airless, and moving in a direction I hadn't chosen. Furthermore, the silence inside the car was not merely the absence of sound; rather, it was the heavy, stretched kind that lives between people who have run out of words, or perhaps never had the right ones to begin with.

They left me at the school gates with nothing but a battered suitcase, a dented tin lunchbox, and a name I no longer trusted. The sun bore down with ruthless indifference, as if intent on burning the shape of their retreat into my memory. And still, I waited naïvely, achingly half-hoping someone might turn back. But hope is a treacherous companion in childhood. It lingers long after reason has packed its bags and left. That day, I came to understand what it meant to be unchosen. And in the hollow silence that followed their departure, I began the quiet, lifelong labour of choosing myself.

As the car pulled away, I caught one final glimpse of my mother, her face framed in the oval rear window of that weathered sixties Beetle. Her hand lifted in a gesture that was meant to be goodbye, but carried all the warmth of a wave to a passing stranger. There was no last-minute embrace, no lingering sorrow in her expression, just a detached farewell, as if I were a parcel being dropped off rather than a son being left behind.

It felt like the velvet curtain falling after the final act on a West End stage, no encore, no cast returning for one last bow. Only the fading echo of applause that never really belonged to you. They left, and I lived.

It wasn't the teary farewell I had imagined, the kind you see in films, where a mother watches her child leave with unwavering sorrow, torn between duty and love. No, this was a distant, mechanical wave, the kind reserved for neighbours, acquaintances, or someone leaving for a routine errand as if sending me off was simply another chore to check off her list.

The sadness was overwhelming, pressing down on me like a weight I couldn't shake off, growing heavier with every mile as the car rattled along the dusty roads, kicking up clouds of red earth that curled and lingered in the heat. The horizon stretched endlessly ahead, and yet, I felt like I was moving further away from everything I had ever known.

For the first time in my life, I was truly alone, no safety net, no familiar voices to anchor me, just a boy unarmed, stepping into a world he couldn't begin to understand. I had no idea what lay ahead, only that I was being sent there because I had failed to be what they wanted me to be.

I imagined the house I had left behind, the walls that had once felt confining now seemed strangely comforting in comparison. My mother's wave, so impersonal, so mechanical, played over in my mind, a silent confirmation that my departure was not an absence to be mourned, but a burden lifted.

But despite the sorrow, there was something else: a quiet, stubborn resolve, a spark buried beneath the grief, whispering that I had to survive this, even if the odds were stacked against me. I had no choice but to face whatever came next, to push forward without the reassurance of home, without the softness of familiarity to fall back on.

I told myself this was a test, a lesson in endurance, a trial I had to face, not just to prove something to them, but to prove something to myself that I could withstand whatever life had planned for me. That I was stronger than they thought, stronger than even I believed.

I had already failed to meet the expectations placed on me at home, had already been dismissed as someone not worth fighting for, but I would not fail this time. I would survive, even if no one expected me to.

Even if no one was watching to see if I did.

***

Tannie (Auntie) Magda van der Merwe was not just a school matron. She had been a storm in a floral apron. Built like an ox but with the heart of a slightly irritated angel, she had roamed the corridors of the school's hostel, striking terror into the hearts of mischief-makers and comfort into those suffering from homesickness. With her iron bun, rolling pin arms, and a pair of beady eyes that could spot a hidden stash of sweets from across the dining hall, she had been both warden and fairy godmother.

Raised on a Free State farm, she had not believed in nonsense, excuses, or weak coffee. Accordingly, when she had told a boy to get up, he had gotten up, whether he had been faking the flu or suffering from actual appendicitis (in which case, she had personally driven him to the hospital while complaining that young people were too soft). Furthermore, her childhood had involved wrangling cattle and even wilder younger siblings, a fact which had explained her unshakable ability to deal with teenage boys who had thought they were cleverer than she was. Spoiler alert: They hadn't been.

Her 'Vetkoek' Fridays had been the stuff of legend. No one had ever figured out exactly how she had managed to produce hundreds of golden, crispy 'Vetkoek' stuffed with curried mince in a single afternoon, but some had suspected supernatural involvement. Even the most rebellious troublemakers had behaved themselves just to stay in her good books for an extra portion. When she had been in a particularly good mood, she might have thrown in a homemade 'koeksister', but only for those who hadn't tested her patience that week.

Tannie Magda's discipline style had been firm but fair. She had never needed to hit, but she had wielded a wooden spoon named 'Ouma' like a military commander pointing out battle formations. If she had caught a boy sneaking out after curfew, she hadn't needed to scream; she had simply raised one eyebrow, and suddenly, he had been confessing every crime he had ever committed, including the time he had stolen a cookie in Grade 3. Her disappointed sigh alone had the power to make grown men rethink their life choices.

Despite her gruffness, she had possessed a heart as big as her collection of sensible shoes. She had quietly slipped extra food onto the trays of struggling students. Not just that, but she had also written letters to parents on behalf of boys who had been too shy. Finally, she had kept a stash of peppermint schnapps purely "for medicinal purposes." (which, coincidentally, had helped her deal with both flu season and staff meetings).

Former students had spoken of her in hushed, reverent tones, and thus the legend of Tannie Magda had lived on. In fact, some had returned years later, successful adults who had still stood up a little straighter when they had heard a spoon clatter. However, the school board had once suggested replacing her with a younger matron. The next day, the entire hostel had united in protest. Ultimately, no one had messed with Tannie Magda. She had not just been a matron; instead, she had been an institution.

Tannie Magda had been my first point of contact when I was unceremoniously dropped off at the school's doorstep, my arrival feeling more like a parcel delivery than the start of an education. After a brief and efficient induction on how the school was run, she led me to my assigned dormitory, both of us dragging my heavy dowry trunk, its weight feeling symbolic of the baggage I carried, both physically and emotionally.

Inside the small, sparsely furnished room, a boy about my age sat on the bed, his left leg bearing deep scars, possibly from a major operation. His posture was relaxed, but the long, jagged lines running down his skin told a different story, one of pain, endurance, and a past I didn't yet understand.

"This is your roommate, Glenn Smith," Tannie Magda announced with forced enthusiasm, as if willing a friendship into existence. *"You two will get along just fine, you're in the same class."*

I smiled weakly. She left, and I was left staring at Glenn's massive scar, unable to look away despite knowing I should.

"I fell off the diving board at the swimming pool," Glenn explained, catching my inquisitive stare. His voice was matter-of-fact, as though he had rehearsed the answer a thousand times before.

"Does it hurt?" I asked, settling onto the chair beside him, still unsure how to navigate this conversation.

"Only sometimes, especially when I walk fast."

That was all he said about it, and it was all I needed to know.

Over time, Glenn and I carved out an easy, unspoken camaraderie, one not forged through dramatic gestures or loud declarations, but through the quiet consistency of showing up. We didn't need to explain ourselves. Our friendship settled into place like an old coat: unassuming, dependable, and exactly what we needed in that strange, cold world.

I helped him when I could, especially with the tasks his injured leg made difficult, carrying things, steadying him when stairs became treacherous, or simply walking beside him so he didn't have to limp alone. In return, Glenn never treated me like an outsider. In a place where everything felt foreign and indifferent, that simple, unwavering acceptance was the greatest gift anyone could offer. It made the unfamiliar less hostile. It made me feel, for the first time in a long time, like I belonged.

***

For the next eight years, I was effectively incarcerated in that boarding school, a place that bore more resemblance to a prison camp than to any nurturing institution of learning. The atmosphere was thick with strict Afrikaans discipline: harsh, unyielding, and enforced with the silent menace of authority.

The cane, our ever-present shadow, was not a metaphor. It was a literal instrument of fear, a thin, leather-bound baton, about two feet long, the same model favoured by the army and police. Male teachers carried it tucked under their arms like a badge of rank, its presence a constant reminder of what would happen if you stepped out of line. It wasn't just a tool. It was a symbol, demanding respect through intimidation.

Any slip, be it academic failure, minor disobedience, or a poorly timed glance, was met with what they called 'six of the best': six sharp lashes across our young backsides, delivered with clinical precision and zero ceremony. It was corporal punishment in its purest form, and though the pain was searing, no one complained. Complaining wasn't just discouraged, it was unthinkable.

The rules were exhaustive, the infractions endless. Untidy or overgrown hair, smudged hands, dirty fingernails, sloppy dormitories, each could warrant punishment, and then there was bedmaking, a daily ordeal turned military ritual. Sheets had to be pulled tight, blankets tucked with surgical accuracy, and a perfect ninety-degree crease pressed along the edge, sharp enough to slice through scrutiny.

The cane, not knowledge or curiosity, ruled that school. It was a place where survival counted more than scholarship. Each day felt less like a step toward the future. Instead, it was more like an endurance test for the present. We learned, yes, but not the lessons we were meant to.

One particular morning remains seared into my memory, not because it was extraordinary, but because it was painfully ordinary, and therein lay the horror. The dormitory bell had rung at 5:45 a.m. sharp, its clang slicing through the early morning silence like a blade. We scrambled from our beds, barefoot on cold cement floors, fumbling in semi-darkness to dress, fold, and prepare for inspection.

That morning, I had made a critical mistake. I had tucked my sheet too shallowly beneath the mattress, and the blanket sagged just slightly at one corner. It was hardly noticeable unless you were looking for it.

Unfortunately, Mr Botha was always looking for it.

He entered like a storm, contained in a suit, tall, broad-shouldered, with the hard, expressionless face of a man who had long since decided kindness was a weakness. The cane was already under his arm, like a second limb. He walked slowly between our beds, tapping his boots against the concrete in rhythm, a sound that made the skin crawl.

When he reached my bed, he stopped. He didn't speak. He simply extended one finger, lifted the sagging corner of the blanket, and let it drop.

"Almeida," he said quietly. "Report after breakfast."

My stomach sank. I couldn't taste the maise porridge that morning. I couldn't think. All I could do was count down the minutes.

After breakfast, I walked to his office, like a man on trial. The door was ajar. He didn't look up as I entered, just gestured to the bench by the wall.

"You know the rules," he said. "Six of the best."

I nodded. No point pleading. No use explaining.

"Touch your toes."

The cane sliced through the air with a terrible elegance, like a conductor's baton summoning pain instead of music. The first lash stole the breath from my lungs. By the third, I was gripping my ankles so tightly my knuckles blanched, every muscle locked in silent resistance, and by the sixth, my vision blurred, my eyes stung, but I refused to let the tears fall. I would not give him that.

When it was over, Mr Botha calmly wiped the cane with a folded handkerchief, as if cleaning a prized instrument, and tucked it beneath his arm with clinical precision.

"Dismissed," he said, without looking at me.

And just like that, it was done. There was no discussion, no reflection, no record. Just the silent understanding that the day would continue as if nothing had happened.

That was the rhythm of our days: pain, silence, obedience. We didn't learn to think. We learned to endure. And yet, somehow, from within those grey, punitive walls, a quiet defiance began to grow. A will to survive. A flicker of identity that no amount of discipline could fully extinguish.

They taught us how to make our beds with military precision, but they never quite learned how to make us surrender.

However, the physical punishments were only the beginning. The environment was a minefield of bullying, where older boys preyed on the younger ones, enforcing an unspoken hierarchy of fear and cruelty. And there were darker shadows that hung over the school, whispers of abuse that were never spoken aloud but were felt in every corner of the dormitories. For many of us, survival meant more than avoiding the cane; it meant navigating the unspoken horrors that lurked beneath the surface.

Through it all, I learned the art of self-preservation not just in body, but in spirit. I became a shadow in the hallways, a ghost in the dorms, expertly shrinking into the background. Attention was dangerous; silence, a shield. The isolation, the blows, the constant threat of punishment became a cruel rhythm I learned to dance to. But even in the darkest corners, a stubborn ember of will refused to die. Somewhere deep within, something kept whispering: *Not yet. Not like this.* I held on to that flicker, a quiet promise to myself that I would rise, not because the world had made it easy, but because I would not let it break me.

In a country where different languages filled the air, survival meant more than just enduring physical challenges; rather, it meant mastering a new language. However, I had no choice but to learn quickly. Indeed, I needed to understand the words around me, not only to know when classmates were plotting pranks, but also to follow teachers' instructions and avoid the sting of the cane, and even to simply ask for food when hunger gnawed at me. Ultimately, language wasn't just a tool; it was a lifeline.

Help, if it could be called that, came in the form of a distant relative, though "help" wasn't quite the right word, and this so-called 'cousin' took more pleasure in bullying me than providing any real assistance. His torment felt like an extension of the trials I already faced, piling on to an already overwhelming sense of isolation. But, as fate would have it, my suffering didn't go unnoticed. One day, a senior pupil caught my cousin in the act and stepped in with a threat I'll never forget. "If I see you bullying your cousin again, I'll break your neck."

After six gruelling months of relentless torment, that senior boy became my most unlikely saviour. His words didn't just halt the bullying; they brought with them a long-forgotten sense of safety. From that day on, Hendrik, affectionately, if not entirely flatteringly, known as "The Pig" thanks to the snorting symphony that accompanied his every laugh, appointed himself my personal bodyguard. It was like having a loyal bulldog with a nasal problem watching over me.

All these challenges, compounded by my learning difficulties, which I didn't even have a name for at the time, pushed me deeper into myself. Years later, I learned I was dyslexic, but back then, all I knew was that words and numbers seemed to conspire against me, leaving me feeling defeated and frustrated. I retreated into the safety of my dormitory, becoming shyer and more introverted with each passing day. Yet, even as I withdrew, a fierce ambition burned inside me, a secret, stubborn belief that one day, I would rise above it all and rule the world.

Home visits were nonexistent, but my schoolmates, sensing my loneliness, took pity on me. Instead of leaving me behind in school during the holidays, they would encourage me to join them on their family farms and homesteads. There, I experienced something I hadn't felt in a long time: warmth, care, and the simple comfort of being part of a family that didn't look at me with disappointment.

Those small moments of kindness from my friends and their families were like beams of light breaking through the dark. They reminded me that, despite everything, I wasn't completely alone. And it was those moments that helped me keep going, even when the road ahead seemed impossibly long.

Among all my schoolmates, Glen stood apart not because he was the loudest or the most athletic, but because he saw me. Truly saw me. While others dismissed my learning difficulties as weaknesses, Glen treated them like a code waiting to be cracked. With quiet patience and a mind sharp as flint, he became both my guide and my anchor.

Under his steady presence, something in me shifted. My attention, once scattered and elusive, began to sharpen. For the first time, I retained the lessons, grasped the concepts, remembered details that used to vanish like mist.

"You just have to write down the trigonometry formulas," Glen would say, his voice calm and assured. "It's like taking a photo then storing it in your brain."

And somehow, miraculously, it worked.

What once felt impossible, distant, unattainable, now became a series of small victories, formulas that stuck, equations that made sense, words that didn't blur together anymore. Glen had unlocked something in me that no teacher, no tutor, no reprimand had ever been able to. He believed I could learn, so I did.

Suddenly, the tides shifted. What had once been pity for the "abandoned child" transformed into something else entirely, an unexpected form of popularity.

The very label that had once made me feel isolated and out of place now became a kind of shield, something that set me apart but not in the way I had feared. Instead of mockery or exclusion, I found acceptance in the most unexpected corners. Classmates who had once been indifferent or distant began to rally around me, their gestures not grand, but meaningful in a way that spoke louder than words.

It was as if my struggle had softened their hearts, as if my presence among them, alone yet determined, had sparked something deeper. In their own way, they sought to protect me, to bring me into the fold rather than let me drift further away.

Apart from Glen, other boys started helping me with my homework. Their rough edges giving way to surprising patience, offering quick explanations, shared notes, and small words of encouragement that made all the difference. And the girls, led by the ever-graceful Candice, with her quiet strength and effortless kindness, took it upon themselves to shape me in the little ways they could.

They smoothed down my unruly hair with gentle hands, straightened my uniform with the precision of caretakers who understood the power of small dignities, and, with knowing smiles, slipped extra snacks into my hands, silent offerings of warmth in a world that often felt indifferent.

They shared the contents of their lunchboxes without ceremony, half a sandwich here, a bruised apple there, the last sweet saved just for me. It wasn't pity. It wasn't charity. It was kinship, offered in the quiet language of children who knew what it meant to go without. In those small, ordinary gestures, I was no longer the outsider, the kid with hand-me-downs and hollow silence. I was one of them. And for the first time in my life, I didn't feel like I was surviving. I felt like I belonged.

The camaraderie at boarding school became my lifeline, an unspoken bond that tethered me to something greater than myself. In a place where hardship and loneliness were common currency, we found solace in each other, our friendships forged in the fire of shared struggle.

Sharing was an unspoken rule, not out of obligation, but because it was how we survived. Food, clothes, advice, whatever we had, we gave. Meals were often meagre, the portions never enough, but what they lacked in size, they made up for in generosity. A bite here, a sip there, sometimes that was all it took to remind me that I wasn't forgotten.

There was something splendid about that sense of community, how we banded together in the face of rigid discipline and an often-harsh environment. Kindness was always at hand, passed along in small gestures, a hand on the shoulder, a smuggled treat, a note of encouragement before a test. It was in these tiny acts of defiance against an unfeeling system that I found my place.

For the first time, I didn't feel like the abandoned child. I felt part of something larger. Those friendships, that warmth, became my shelter from the storm.

Now, as I look back, the scars of those years remain. Some are physical, but most are hidden deep within, reminders of the battles I fought and the pain I endured, but every scar is a testament to my resilience. They remind me that I faced every challenge, survived every hardship, and came out the other side.

The school may have been meant to break me, but in the end, it only sharpened me. They may have sent me away, but I returned forged, not broken. No cane, no silence, no cruel indifference could smother the fire in me. I came back not just to survive, but to rise.

Chapter 10:
A Banker Without a Bank.

And then there was Candice. The girl with the round face framed by golden blonde hair, her piercing blue eyes carrying a light that seemed to pierce straight through the weight of the world I carried on my shoulders. She was the kind of pretty that left an imprint in your memory, not just because of her looks, but because of the way she moved through life with an ease, a confidence that made the mundane seem remarkable. Candice was the daughter of a kettle farmer, a detail I learned much later, and she boarded in the girls' dormitory, a stately brick-faced building with ivy creeping up its sides, forever separated from the boys' quarters by a high, unyielding wall. Males and females were like oil and water in those days, strictly segregated, their interactions limited to the classroom or the playground, where watchful eyes ensured nothing improper ever occurred.

For reasons that still baffle me to this day, Candice took a shine to me. I was a new arrival then, still adjusting to what felt like a prison sentence, six months into my so-called "education" in that institution of rigid rules and harsher realities. I was the outsider, the awkward boy with a name that didn't quite fit the mould and a demeanour that made me an easy target for the bullies prowling the corridors.

I remember the day our paths truly crossed, the day she stepped into my story like a guardian angel with steel in her spine. It was a grey, unremarkable afternoon, the kind where the sky hung low and heavy, pressing the world into something dull and lifeless, and yet, in the monotony of that day, something happened that would carve itself into the marrow of my memory forever.

One of the boys, bigger, stronger, and meaner, the kind who fed on fear and sharpened his teeth on the weak, decided that my existence needed a reminder of its insignificance. With a shove, careless yet deliberate, he sent me reeling. The world tilted, gravity snatching me before I could even brace for it. My body hit the stairs hard, tumbling down in a helpless sprawl. Cold stone bit into my knees, my palms, my ribs, every jagged edge of the staircase marking its claim on me. Pain flared hot and bright, a wildfire licking through my limbs, but humiliation burned even hotter.

Laughter echoed around me, sharp, cruel, the kind that gnawed at whatever scraps of dignity I had left. I stayed where I had fallen, stunned, breathless, waiting for the world to settle. But before I could even lift my head, she was there: Candice.

She appeared like a storm breaking over a drought-ridden land, sudden and fierce, her presence cutting through the jeering crowd like a blade. There was no hesitation in the way she stepped between my tormentor and me, no fear in the way she squared her shoulders, meeting his smug cruelty with something infinitely stronger.

It was in that moment that I understood, there are some people the world cannot break. And when they choose to stand for you, it changes everything.

As I struggled to gather myself, I saw her. Candice. She moved swiftly, her steps purposeful, her gaze sharp as a blade. She knelt beside me without hesitation, her delicate fingers dabbing at the blood trickling from my knee with a handkerchief that smelled faintly of lavender. Her touch was gentle, yet her voice carried a weight that silenced the crowd gathering around us. Turning to my aggressor, she spoke with a calm fury that left no room for argument.

"If I ever see you or any of you," she added, her gaze sweeping across the group of onlookers, "doing that to Gabriel again, I'll tell my brother to break your neck."

There was something about the way she said it, measured, unwavering, that made everyone believe she meant it. And maybe she did. From that moment on, the bullying stopped altogether, as if her words had cast some kind of protective spell over me.

That evening, I returned to the dormitory with the blood-stained handkerchief in hand. It was a token of kindness, a lifeline in a sea of hostility, and I treated it with the reverence it deserved. I washed it carefully in the communal bathroom, hung it over the steel frame of my bed to dry, and handed it back to her the next morning.

"You keep it," she said with a smile that crinkled the corners of her eyes. "A souvenir from your protector."

And just like that, an extraordinary bond was forged, a connection that defied the barriers of age, gender, and circumstance. It wasn't just gratitude I felt for her; it was something deeper, a recognition of a kindred spirit in the most unexpected of places.

A few days later, she surprised me again. It was during lunch break when she pressed a crisp one-rand note into my hand. I stared at it, bewildered, unsure of what to say.

"Here," she said, her tone casual but her eyes warm. "Take this and go to the cinema on Saturday. Enjoy yourself on me."

I was speechless. No one had ever done anything like that for me before. My parents didn't believe in pocket money; every cent was accounted for in our household, and frivolities like movies were out of the question. Yet here was Candice, a girl who barely knew me, offering me a chance to experience something joyful, something normal.

It wasn't just the generosity that struck me. It was the way she made me feel seen, as if I mattered in a way I hadn't dared to believe before. From that day forward, she became more than a classmate, more than a friend. She was my protector, my confidante, and my reminder that even in the darkest corners of life, there could be light.

Our bond would endure the test of time, etched into my memory like the scent of lavender on that handkerchief, fragile yet unbreakable, simple yet profound. Candice didn't just change my life; she reminded me of the kindness that exists in the world, waiting for the right moment to reveal itself.

***

The summer school holidays had settled into their first week, a six-week stretch spanning Christmas and New Year. For most kids, it was a season of celebration, family gatherings, and the kind of joy that lingered in the air like the scent of pine needles and festive feasts. For me, it was a bleak expanse of empty days and echoing silence. There was no trip home in sight, no letters, no phone calls, no explanation. My family, it seemed, had simply forgotten my existence. Or perhaps, they'd chosen to. The reasons didn't matter much when the outcome was the same.

The prospect of wandering the barren corridors of the dormitory stretched before me like a punishment wrapped in silence. In one sense, it was a relief. The bullies were gone, scattered back to their homes, leaving behind only the echo of their cruelty. No shoves, no threats, no orders barked through clenched teeth. Just peace, a hollow, eerie kind of peace.

But the quiet… the quiet had teeth. It clawed at me in the dark, gnawed at my resolve, and carried the faint, metallic scent of damp stone and old dust. At night, the old building seemed to inhale and exhale with its own uneasy breath. Floorboards moaned, pipes whispered, and I imagined ghosts of boys long gone pacing beside me, their footsteps cold enough to raise the hair on my arms. I locked my door like a ritual, stacking chairs against it until the wood groaned under the pressure, as if wood and willpower could hold back the things I couldn't name. I wouldn't dare leave my room until dawn smudged the windows with light and reminded me I hadn't vanished.

Even nature turned against me. The bathroom down the corridor became a place of shadows and imagined terrors. I held my breath and my bladder, counting the hours until sunrise. Because in that lonely silence, courage had a curfew.

But there were small mercies, tiny rebellions against my circumstances that kept me sane. I savoured the extra hour in bed each morning, no longer forced to compete with my dorm mates for a spot in the bathroom or the last slice of toast at breakfast. The dining hall, deserted as it was, became a kind of sanctuary. Meals were served at the usual times, artfully arranged on the kitchen counter, and covered with a mosquito net, as if some phantom chef had prepared them in secret. I never saw the cook, but the simple and sufficient food kept me going. For a thirteen-year-old boy, it was enough. Barely.

The days bled into each other, a slow, monotonous rhythm of solitude. I spent my hours at the pool, kicking a football aimlessly around the empty soccer stadium, or hunched over my desk, drawing. The pencil was my escape, as each line on the page became a step into a world that wasn't mine but could be, if only I imagined hard enough. Since television hadn't yet arrived in the country, the radio was my constant companion. Specifically, I tuned in to the local rock 'n roll station, which served as a kind of rebellious echo of the UK's pirate station, Radio Caroline. It was the soundtrack of my isolation, each beat a reminder that there was a bigger world out there, somewhere beyond these walls.

Occasionally, the headmaster or the maintenance man would make their rounds in a half-hearted patrol, more for the sake of appearance than genuine concern. They moved through the halls like ghosts haunting a place they had long stopped caring for, their presence fleeting, their purpose routine. A perfunctory glance here, a cursory nod there, as if ensuring the walls were still standing and that I, the forgotten boy, had not yet faded into the dust.

Their interactions were sparse and awkward, "hi" from the headmaster, tossed in my direction like loose change, or a gruff, "hmm" from the maintenance man, a sound that could have meant anything or nothing at all. They came and went, never lingering long enough to shatter the quiet loneliness that had settled around me like an old, familiar coat. Their presence confirmed that I existed, but never quite enough to make me feel seen.

And then, there was Tannie Magda. She would appear like a whisper of warmth in the cold, slipping through the margins of my solitude with her quiet, unwavering kindness. She never made a grand spectacle of it, never fussed or fawned, but every now and then, she'd arrive with something small yet significant. A special tart, baked with the kind of care that turned flour and sugar into comfort. A treat, wrapped in simple paper but carrying the weight of a reminder that I was not completely forgotten.

She never said much, but she didn't have to. Her presence alone was an unspoken assurance: I see you. I remember you. *You are not alone.*

And in a place where being invisible had become my daily existence, that meant everything.

Then, one afternoon, as I sat at my desk sketching, the door to my room swung open without warning. My heart leapt, caught between fear and hope. I turned, expecting what? A ghost? A punishment? Instead, I saw him: Ian Nel, none other than Candice's older brother.

Ian was a figure of legend, the kind of boy every other boy wanted to be, and every girl wanted to know. Tall and broad-shouldered, he seemed to carry the world effortlessly on his back. He was the school's head prefect, the captain of the rugby team, the leader of the school band, a man of endless accolades. In his final year of high school, he'd already achieved what seemed impossible: a driver's license, a badge of adulthood few could boast at the time. Standing in the doorway, he looked like a hero straight out of one of the adventure novels I used to dream of reading.

"Get ready," he said, his voice firm but not unkind. "I'm taking you to our home."

I blinked at him, my pencil frozen mid-stroke. "But…" I began, my voice barely above a whisper. Leaving the school grounds without permission was tantamount to desertion, a crime punishable by swift and severe consequences.

"Don't worry," he interrupted, his tone leaving no room for argument. "The principal's been notified."

His words hung in the air, heavy with authority. I wanted to protest, to question why he was doing this, but something in his demeanour silenced me. There was no malice in his eyes, only a quiet determination. And for the first time in weeks, maybe months, I felt something stir in me, a flicker of hope, fragile but persistent.

Without another word, I set down my pencil and stood. For the first time in what felt like forever, I allowed myself to believe that maybe, just maybe, I wasn't as forgotten as I'd feared. Ian's presence, commanding yet comforting, was enough to anchor me in that fragile hope. And so, with nothing but the clothes on my back and a swirl of emotions in my chest, I followed him out of the dormitory and into his car.

The drive to the farm felt like an escape, as though we were leaving behind the suffocating weight of the school and heading toward a world I could barely imagine. The first stretch of the journey was smooth, the asphalt ribboning out before us under a cerulean sky. But halfway there, Ian veered onto a dusty, red-earth road that cut through a barren, sun-drenched valley.

The landscape stretched endlessly, stark yet beautiful, with occasional patches of farmland breaking up the monotony. The fields, dotted with grazing cattle and the occasional windmill, seemed to whisper promises of peace and freedom. The car's windows were down, and the dry air carried the earthy scent of the countryside, a sharp contrast to the sterile dormitories I had left behind.

When we finally arrived, the farm stood like a vision out of another life. The house, an expansive Colonial-style structure with wide verandas and tall sash windows, was a testament to understated elegance. Its whitewashed walls gleamed in the sunlight, and the scent of blooming jacaranda trees wafted on the breeze. Ian led me inside, his pace steady, his demeanour calm. The cool interior was a haven from the heat; the wooden floors were polished to a mirror-like shine. He guided me upstairs to a bright, airy room with tall windows that opened onto a view of the sprawling farm below.

"This is your room," Ian said, his voice steady and warm. "Make yourself comfortable. I'll go get Candice."

For a moment, I stood there in stunned silence, taking in my surroundings. The room was far more luxurious than anything I had ever known, clean, inviting, and filled with light. The view from the windows was breathtaking: rolling green fields stretching to the horizon, dotted with livestock, and framed by distant hills. It was a world so far removed from the stark dormitories and their suffocating walls that I felt like I had stepped into a dream.

Before dinner, Candice appeared, radiant and full of energy. She swept me into a tour of the house and the farm, her excitement infectious. She showed me the stables, where sleek horses whinnied softly, and the fields, where workers tended to the crops with practised ease. The farm was alive, vibrant with activity and purpose, and I couldn't help but be impressed by the sheer scale and beauty of it all.

The Nel family welcomed me with a warmth I hadn't anticipated. Mrs Nel, kind-eyed and perpetually smiling, handed me a bundle of fresh clothes, comfortable shoes, and toiletries as though I were her own son.

"You'll need these," she said, her voice gentle but firm, her hands lingering on my shoulders as if to reassure me. Mr Nel, tall and broad-shouldered, observed me with a calculating but not unkind gaze.

"I hope you're enjoying yourself," he said repeatedly, as though trying to gauge whether I truly felt at ease.

And then there was Candice, vibrant, glowing, and unapologetically delighted by my presence. She hovered nearby, her laughter filling the air, her gestures animated as she guided me from place to place.

It was all so perfect, so surreal, that I found it hard to believe. After so many years of feeling invisible, their kindness felt almost foreign. And yet, I couldn't help but bask in it, allowing myself to soak in the warmth and affection I had long since given up hoping for.

Mealtimes were perhaps the most striking contrast to my upbringing. At the Nel family table, there was no silence, no tension, no quiet dread of saying the wrong thing. Instead, there was chatter and laughter, the kind that spilled over like a bubbling brook, light and unrestrained. Their dialogue danced between Afrikaans and English, their voices rising and falling in a symphony of familial connection. They were mindful of me, ensuring I understood every word. "Do you understand?" they would ask, their tones patient and inclusive, repeating themselves if necessary. It wasn't just a question. It was an invitation, a way of drawing me into their world, making sure I felt like I belonged.

For the first time in as long as I could remember, I felt not only seen but truly cared for. The Nels had opened their home and their hearts to me, a boy they barely knew, and in doing so, they gave me something I hadn't realised I was missing: the quiet assurance that I mattered. As I sat at their table, surrounded by laughter and the scent of freshly baked bread, I couldn't help but think that maybe, just maybe, this was what family was supposed to feel like.

***

A few days into my stay, I found myself gathered around the massive dining room table, a piece of furniture that bore the weight of both time and purpose. Its thick pine top, scarred with deep grooves and the faint stains of past meals, told the story of a life well-lived. The carved legs, sturdy and unwavering, had stood witness to decades of conversations, laughter, and the occasional argument. But this table was more than just a place to eat. It was a multipurpose workhorse space where Mrs Nel stitched new garments, where Candice sketched out her latest designs, where dead gazelles were skinned and butchered with practised efficiency. And today, it had been transformed into something else entirely: a counting house.

At the centre of the table lay a mountain of coins and notes, a shimmering heap of wealth poured out from a half-dozen metal boxes that Mr Nel had collected over the week. I had never seen so much money in my life. The sheer volume of it, stacks of silver, piles of copper, crisp banknotes fanned out as a deck of cards, left me staring in wide-eyed wonder.

Everyone around the table seemed to know what they were doing, their hands moving with the ease of routine. I, on the other hand, was completely at a loss.

Sensing my confusion, Candice leaned over and whispered, "Pick out all the small, dark coins and set them aside."

I obeyed without question, carefully sifting through the pile as the rest of the family sorted and counted with precision. It was a strangely rhythmic process, the soft clinking of coins and the rustling of banknotes forming a steady, hypnotic cadence. When the sorting was complete, Mrs Nel meticulously placed the coins and notes into separate bags, marking down the totals in what looked like an official bank deposit slip.

That afternoon, we loaded up the car and drove into town, making our way to the bank. I watched as Mr Nel handed over the neatly packaged money to the teller, exchanging a few words before receiving a small orange booklet in return. The entire transaction baffled me. Why would anyone just give all their money to the bank? What if they lost it? What if the bank decided not to give it back?

At dinner that night, my curiosity got the better of me. "Why did you give all the money to the bank?" I asked hesitantly.

Mr Nel set down his fork and gave me a thoughtful look, as though deciding how best to explain. "You give money to the bank," he began, "and the bank lends that money to people who need it. In return, you earn interest." He paused, gauging my reaction. Seeing my puzzled expression, he continued, "Interest is money the bank pays you, just for keeping your money there. The more you save, the more you earn."

He reached into his pocket and pulled out the small orange booklet, flipping it open to reveal neatly written figures. "Every now and then," he went on, "the bank adds the interest to your account, and you can see your money grow." He tapped the page lightly before looking up at me. "Do you understand?"

I nodded slowly, though scepticism still gnawed at the edges of my thoughts. It sounded almost too good to be true. Money that multiplies on its own? Just by sitting in a bank? It felt like some kind of sorcery, a trick of numbers I had yet to understand. And yet, the more I turned the idea over in my mind, the more it fascinated me.

If this system truly worked, then maybe just maybe I could harness it to my advantage.

At school, my classmates were perpetually broke, always scrounging for loose change to buy sweets, catch a movie, or impress a girl with a fleeting gesture of extravagance. They borrowed endlessly, scraping by on the generosity or gullibility of others. Watching their constant need, an idea began to take shape. A spark of opportunity, waiting to be ignited.

At the end of the holiday, as a token of appreciation for the work I had done around the farm, mucking out the stables, rounding up cattle and sheep, and counting the week's earnings, Mr Nel handed me a crisp five-rand note. It was more money than I had ever owned at one time, and I held it as though it were something sacred.

Instead of spending it recklessly, I decided to put Mr Nel's lesson into practice. I changed the note into five one-rand coins and, little by little, began lending them out to my schoolmates. For every rand I loaned, I charged an extra fifty cents in interest. At first, I wasn't sure if they would actually pay me back, but to my amazement, they did eagerly and without question. It worked!

Before long, my small operation flourished. Coins found their way back to me in greater numbers than I had lent, a steady stream of repayments laced with the sweet bonus of interest. My schoolmates, always eager for an advance, never questioned the extra cost, happy to trade tomorrow's money for today's pleasure.

Each night, after lights-out, Glenn would snore blissfully into his pillow, entirely oblivious to the silent world around him. Meanwhile, I would reach beneath my mattress, my fingers gliding over the familiar groove in the hollow bed frame. With the ease of a seasoned banker, I slid open my makeshift vault. Then, I slipped the day's earnings inside, my movements precise, my breath measured.

Then came the sound, the soft, unmistakable chime of metal against metal. A whisper of wealth in the darkness. A lullaby composed not in notes, but in coins, the currency of the clever, the hymn of the quietly ambitious.

It was a sound only I knew, a secret only I held. And as the weight of my fortune grew, so too did the quiet satisfaction that hummed beneath my ribs.

Success, after all, had a melody. And I had learned to listen.

But success, I soon learned, had weight, literal weight.

At first, the growing stash was a source of pride, proof that my venture was working, that I had built something entirely my own. But as the coins stacked higher, so did my unease. My once-light bed frame, which I could shift effortlessly to sweep the dust beneath it, now groaned under the burden of my small yet formidable fortune. Moving it became a struggle. The simple act of making my bed carried the risk of an accidental metallic clink, a sound that could betray everything.

And if I had noticed, who was to say that someone else wouldn't?

What if a prefect, in one of their dreaded room inspections, decided to check beneath the bed? What if a dormitory raid uncovered the weight of my ambitions, rattling in a pile of incriminating silver? I wasn't just a schoolboy with a clever idea anymore. I was a banker without a bank. A financier without security.

I needed a safer option. I needed another place to hide the money. I needed one of those orange books.

Mr. Nel carried the bank books with a reverence that made them seem almost mythical. Ultimately, those little volumes held more than just numbers; they held protection. For, as I'd learned from his quiet lessons, real wealth wasn't merely about what you possessed; rather, it was about where you kept it.

But until I could get my hands on one of those elusive orange ledgers, I had to think fast.

My newfound fortune was growing steadily, undeniably, and my bed frame was no longer an option. One wrong move, one curious prefect, one errant clink of coin at the wrong time, and it could all come crashing down.

So, I turned to what I knew best. The school had its hidden corners, places most students never thought twice about. My duties often took me beyond the usual haunts, granting me access to spaces that were both forgotten and forbidden.

The pump room beneath the swimming pool came to mind first. Damp, humming with the churn of old machinery, thick with the sting of chlorine, the kind of place no one lingered longer than necessary. I knew every inch of it from mornings spent skimming leaves off the water and scrubbing tiles until they shone. A dark recess behind the pump… perhaps?

Then there was the science lab, locked cabinets, shelves of half-used chemicals, forgotten tools collecting dust in shadowed corners. If I could find the right drawer, the right crevice, it might just serve as my vault.

Then, there was the woodwork workshop. The scent of varnish clung to the air, with sawdust drifting like golden smoke beneath the beams. Within its walls stood old lockers and hollow workbenches, surrounded by shadows no one looked too closely into. Yet, in that obscurity, I saw all possibilities.

Still, I hesitated. No place felt truly safe. Not yet.

The more my stash grew, the more I realised hiding it wasn't enough. A wooden drawer or a dusty corner wouldn't cut it anymore. I needed something more. Something official.

But until I could walk into a bank and sign my name into one of those orange books, I'd have to keep running the numbers, weighing the risks, staying one step ahead of discovery.

Because if there's one thing I'd learned about money, it's this: The moment people know you have it, they start thinking of ways to take it.

I needed one of those damn orange books, the kind that transformed loose change into something real, something that mattered. But that was a dream for another day.

For now, I needed something sturdier. A metal box.

The kind I'd once seen at the Nels' house, the one that had spilled its contents like a broken dam, banknotes fluttering across the table like startled birds. Sturdy. Unassuming. Built to keep prying hands out and precious things in.

That would do for now.

But even a box needed a place. A hiding spot so perfect, so cleverly chosen, even I would hesitate before retrieving my own fortune. Because money, I was learning, wasn't just about having it. It was about keeping it.

Safe.
Secure.
Untouchable.

Until the day came when I could walk into a bank, sign my name, and claim one of those orange books…

I would settle for steel and secrecy. A vault of my own making. And so, one by one, I tested my options, slipping into potential hiding places under the guise of my usual routines. Scrubbing floors. Fetching supplies. Running errands. Every location had to be tested, its weaknesses measured against its promise.

Would anyone linger here? Could someone stumble upon it by accident? Could I retrieve it without drawing suspicion?

Each place whispered its own possibilities. None felt quite right.

Until, finally, I found myself at Patel's. And there in that cluttered, unremarkable corner of town, the next piece of my plan began to take shape.

On our next trip into town, while my classmates rushed toward the cinema, I turned down a quieter street, making my way toward the small Indian-run shop that sold everything imaginable. Patel's was a place of organised chaos, a narrow storefront packed to the rafters with an eclectic mix of goods. The scent of spices mingled with the metallic tang of hardware tools, and somewhere in the back, the faint melody of an old Bollywood tune played from a crackling radio. Patel's was the kind of place that time had politely ignored. Wedged between the town's butcher and the barber, both of whom had long since modernised, Mr Patel's shop remained stubbornly untouched by progress. The peeling sign above the door read "Patel's Sundries & Supplies," though no one could quite define what *sundries* meant anymore.

The brass bell above the door gave a tired jingle as I stepped inside, releasing a scent so distinctive it felt like crossing into another world: cardamom, mothballs, paraffin, and something sweetly metallic like rusted tin toys and memories.

It wasn't just a shop. It was a museum curated by a man who collected the odd, the old, and the oddly useful.

Along the cramped aisles, you'd find ancient tins of Dubbin shoe polish, next to half-melted candles, boxes of thumbtacks from a brand that no longer existed, and cassette tapes labelled in languages I couldn't read. Near the back, there was a dusty birdcage that had never known a bird, an army helmet from a war no one talked about, and a set of porcelain dentures displayed like fine china, no explanation, no price tag.

Mr Patel himself stood behind the wooden counter like a guardian of forgotten things, rearranging a stack of yellowing receipts and old bolts. He barely looked up when I entered, just gave a curt nod and went on sorting through a crate filled with padlocks and tangled extension cords.

I moved slowly through the aisles, not in search of anything specific but because Patel's was a place that rewarded wandering.

And that's when I saw them.

Stacked near the back, beneath a faded poster of Mahatma Gandhi and a shelf of mismatched torch batteries, sat a neat pile of small metal cash boxes. Hinged, matte grey, each with a tiny key taped to its lid.

They didn't look like much. No fancy logos. No velvet lining. But they were sturdy. Practical. Quiet.

Exactly what I needed.

I picked one up, feeling the cool weight in my hands, not heavy, but dense enough to mean something. I turned it over, checking the corners, the lock, the hinges. I could already see it: lined with coins, folded notes, tucked away in a place only I would know.

Mr Patel's eyes flicked toward me, bright and knowing, like he'd seen this scene play out before. "Good choice," he said, tapping the side of his nose. "Keeps what's yours… yours."

I didn't say a word. Just nodded.

Because he understood, and now so did I.

I tucked it swiftly into my backpack, hidden beneath my school sweater, and left the shop without another word.

As I stepped back into the sweltering afternoon, the weight of the metal box pressed reassuringly against my back. It wasn't just an object. It was a statement. A declaration of intent.

Now, I had a safe.

The next challenge? Finding a way to secure it permanently.

***

For the next week or so, my brain toggled between two vastly different concerns, half-listening to geography lessons (something about plate tectonics, maybe?) and meticulously strategising the ultimate hiding spot for my growing stash. Every spare moment was spent mentally mapping out potential locations, dismissing each one like a paranoid squirrel unsatisfied with its acorn burial site.

Before I knew it, pool-cleaning duty was back on the schedule. With a dramatic sigh worthy of an overworked labourer, I dragged the cleaning equipment out of the pump room. That's when I saw it, a small electrical distribution board, bolted to the wall with thick angle brackets. My gaze sharpened.

And then, jackpot. A narrow gap, barely visible, lurking between the board and the wall. Just wide enough to slide in my precious money box. My heart did a little victory jig. A slow grin crept across my face, the kind of grin that villains in movies flash just before unveiling their master plan.

Perfect. I whispered it under my breath, savouring the triumph. This was it. The ultimate hiding place. Safe, discreet, genius. What could possibly go wrong?

Every time pool-cleaning duty rolled around, my pockets transformed into miniature treasure chests, bulging with coins destined for the almighty money box. At times, I half-expected my pocket stitching to wave the white flag, surrendering to the sheer weight of my newfound fortune, and sending a cascade of coins clattering across the schoolyard, an unintentional charity event for my classmates.

Luckily, school uniforms back then were built to withstand the apocalypse, or at least the rough-and-tumble life of a student janitor with an accidental side hustle. The heavy-duty stitching held firm, sparing me the embarrassment of a rogue coin shower and allowing me to waddle my way to the money box like a well-funded pirate.

For months, my little operation ran as smoothly as a well-oiled vending machine. The money box grew heavier with every pool-cleaning session, while my bed frame, once a sturdy structure groaning under the weight of my original stash, began to feel suspiciously lightweight. Life was good. But, as with all good things, trouble was on the horizon, winter was coming. And with it, the dreaded seasonal pool closure.

One fateful afternoon, as I peered out of my dormitory window, my stomach did an Olympic-level dive. The pool area was a war zone of workers draining water, tearing up loose tiles, and painting handrails. My pool. My stash site. A horrified mumble escaped my lips: "Oh no… they should have told me." As if I were some kind of secret shareholder in the pool's existence.

Panic set in. I needed a new plan fast. This wasn't just about convenience; this was about survival. Or at the very least, saving my life's savings.

So, under the cover of darkness, I sprang into action. I snuck down to the ground floor, climbed, rather ungracefully, through the dining room window, and made my way toward the pump room. The space was a chaotic sprawl of building materials, rogue tools, and enough sharp debris to turn any intrusion into a trial by fire. My boots crunched over loose gravel with a sound that seemed to echo like a gunshot in the silent house. Sure enough, I caught my foot on a slab of rubble, hitting the floor hard and skinning my knee. As the sting of blood bloomed against my trousers, I muttered a string of words that would have made a sailor nod in approval. Yet, the biting cold of the floor didn't stop me; I pressed on, fuelled by a frantic mix of sheer determination and financial self-preservation.

Finally, I reached my prize. With one swift, victorious movement, I liberated the money box from its precarious hideout, snatching it away from the looming chaos of construction.

Years later, I would come to appreciate Murphy's Law: *Anything that can go wrong, will go wrong.* But in that moment, I had no time for philosophy, only stealth.

Returning to the dormitory in deafening silence, my backpack weighed down by my hard-earned loot, I made my way to my next hiding spot. The linen cupboard. It was a backup plan I'd considered before, though it came with one annoying drawback: I needed to find the damn key every time I wanted access. But desperate times call for inconvenient measures.

With a deep breath, I slid the money box under the plenum of the cupboard, stepped back, and whispered to myself:

Let's hope this one doesn't come with a construction crew.

***

It was no longer just a passing thought. It had become an obsession. That little orange booklet wasn't just a collection of numbers; it was power. It was the difference between some kid hoarding loose change in a sock and a real player with a bank account. It was the key to transforming my carefully guarded stash from a fragile, dormitory-bound secret into something permanent, something untouchable.

Because as long as my money remained hidden in makeshift nooks and crannies, it was at risk, at risk of discovery, of theft, of the chaos that was dormitory life. A bank account, though? That was security. That was legitimacy. That was wealth, protected by the very same system Mr Nel had spoken so reverently about over dinner that night.

There was a problem, though. The rules were infuriatingly simple: only adults could open bank accounts. And as far as the world was concerned, I was just a thirteen-year-old boy with no business having savings of my own. But rules were meant to be… worked around. And that didn't change the fact that I had money. More than most of the boys at school. Maybe even more than some of the teachers, if we were being honest.

I wasn't about to let bureaucracy stand in the way of my financial empire.

So, I did what any ambitious thirteen-year-old would do: I observed. I started watching, listening, gathering information like a pickpocket in a crowded marketplace. I studied the privileged older boys, sons of well-off families whose parents had set up accounts for them. They strolled into town on Saturdays, withdrew pocket money with the casual ease of men who didn't have to dig through mattress seams for spare change.

I asked careful questions, never too direct, never too eager. But no matter how much I learned, one frustrating truth remained: I needed an adult to vouch for me.

Marching into a bank alone and demanding a savings account would be ridiculous. No banker in their right mind would hand an orange booklet to a scrawny thirteen-year-old with a hopeful grin and pockets full of suspiciously acquired coins.

But that didn't mean it was impossible.

And that's when my focus shifted.

I started paying attention to new details. Who among the older boys had accounts? How exactly did they get them? Was there a loophole? Could I find an adult, a trusted, reasonable adult, to unknowingly assist me in my mission?

That's when the idea took root: Mr. Nel.

Of all the adults in my world, he was the only one who had ever spoken to me about money, as if I actually had a future. He wasn't just another teacher rattling off lectures. No, he had explained things. Taught me about interest. About saving. About the system itself. He treated me like someone with potential, not just another kid lost in the shuffle.

If anyone could help me, it was him.

But I had to be smart. I couldn't just blurt it out like some desperate street urchin. No, I had to plant the idea in his mind like a master tactician. Make him believe the thought was his own.

So, I waited.

The next time I was invited to the farm, I steered the conversation toward savings, toward banks, toward the importance of securing one's earnings. I nodded at all the right moments, played the role of the eager young pupil, letting him talk himself into the very idea I needed him to have.

And then, when the moment was just right, I casually set the bait.

"I've been thinking," I said, pushing a piece of bread around my plate with practised nonchalance. "You know how you said the bank pays you interest for keeping money there?"

Mr Nel nodded, chewing thoughtfully.

"Well… what if I wanted to start saving properly? You always say it's important to think ahead. Wouldn't it be smart for me to have an account, too? Even if I'm young?"

I held my breath.

He set down his fork, narrowed his eyes, and studied me for a long moment. My heart pounded. And then, finally, he nodded.

"That's a wise thought, Gabriel," he said slowly. "A very wise thought."

The next day, we drove into town, my heart thudding with the kind of anticipation usually reserved for secret agents on their first mission. I stepped into the bank, trying to look as serious and financially responsible as a thirteen-year-old could.

With what I hoped was the confidence of a seasoned investor, I slid a five-Rand note across the counter. It was a small fortune in my world, a testament to months of careful hoarding, strategic hiding, and mildly criminal levels of determination. And then, finally, the teller slid it back to me: one of those damn orange books. The paper felt unexpectedly thick, almost impossibly heavy in my palm, its cheap binding vibrating with the gravity of a life-changing contract. I gripped it tightly, my knuckles turning white, resisting the urge to let out an unprofessional whoop of victory. I had done it. In that simple, tactile exchange, the abstract walls of the world had parted. I was in the system.

No more stashing coins behind electrical boards or risking my life climbing through windows. No more dormitory chaos threatening my fortune. I was officially a man of finance.

Well… at least, that's how it felt.

Chapter 11:
The Silent Hand of Power.

The classroom's crackly PA system sputtered to life midway through an already dull history lesson, startling me like a slap on the back of the neck. Static crackled. Then came the voice, dry, deliberate, and vaguely amused.

"The principal would like to see… Almeida."

Time stopped. My spine stiffened. Heads turned.

Great... here comes the cane again.

My first instinct? Panic sharp and immediate, like ice water down the back. What had I done? Nothing came to mind. Which was worse. At this school, guilt was a luxury. Innocence simply meant they hadn't caught you yet. Here, crimes were optional; punishments were mandatory.

As the teacher nodded me toward the door without so much as a glance, my legs moved on their own. Each step toward the hallway felt like walking deeper into a trap. The classroom door closed behind me with a soft click that sounded, in my ears, like a jail cell locking.

The corridor stretched ahead long, polished, echoing. My shoes tapped against the floor like a ticking clock counting down to judgment. The flickering overhead lights cast long shadows that moved like watchful eyes. Every classroom I passed seemed suddenly louder, more alive, as if the rest of the school were carrying on in blissful ignorance while I marched to my doom.

I kept my gaze down, avoiding the eyes of passing teachers. Some barely looked up. Others gave me that brief, knowing glance, the kind that said, *better you than me.*

By the time I reached the principal's office, my palms were sweating, my pulse drumming in my ears. I stood before the door for a moment, hand hovering just above the handle, wondering if I should knock… or run.

The principal's secretary, whose face looked like it had never known the concept of joy, ushered me into the office. I braced for impact.

But instead of the usual scolding, my eyes landed on an old woman, sitting across from the principal's desk. Short, frail, her hair streaked with grey. I squinted.

Wait… was that…?

My mother.

I hadn't seen her in over six years, and now here she was like a plot twist I hadn't signed up for. She stood up, wrapped me in a hug, and for a brief moment, I let myself enjoy it. But something about it felt… off. Like hugging a friendly apparition. Warm, yet eerily distant.

Then she dropped another bomb.

Pointing to a man slouched in the corner, she said, "That's Uncle Albert. You'll be staying with him when you leave school at the end of the year."

I turned to look at him.

Albert looked back, his bloodshot eyes squinting through the haze of a life misspent. His face was a roadmap of ruin etched with deep-set wrinkles carved by years of chain-smoking, hard drinking, and the kind of choices that never make it into polite conversation.

His yellowed fingers, trembling slightly, drummed against his knee in a rhythm known only to old regrets. The collar of his shirt sagged like surrender, and the stale tang of beer and bitter memories clung to him like a second skin.

He gave me the slow once-over eyes, dragging from head to toe not with judgment, but with that weary indifference of someone who's seen better people fall harder. His expression hovered somewhere between faint curiosity and quiet disappointment, as if he'd just uncovered an unpaid bar tab written in my name.

And then, like a ghost slipping back into the walls, my mother disappeared. No goodbye. No explanation. No drawn-out emotion.

Just a plastic bag of biscuits left on the desk.

Her parting gift. A silent, crumbling metaphor for affection she'd never learned to say aloud.

I stared at the biscuits, unsure whether to eat them or cry.

That was it? That was the grand reunion? No sudden declaration of maternal love? No "Pack your bags, you're coming home" moment? Nope. Just Uncle Albert and a bag of biscuits.

I sighed. My dreams were officially shattered. Once again, I was on my own, only this time, with a wrinkled-faced, chain-smoking, beer-scented guardian who looked at me like I was a burden he hadn't asked for.

For the next four months, I dreaded the inevitable day when I would have to say goodbye to the sanctuary of my dormitory, trading it for the unknown horrors of Uncle Albert's residence. The uncertainty gnawed at me, but in the back of my mind, there was always the safety net of the Nel family. Candice's kind words echoed like a lifeline: "When you leave here, remember to call on us if you ever need anything."

Then, on a warm afternoon, just a few weeks after completing my high school exams, the moment arrived. After a tearful goodbye to Candice, Tannie Magda, and school buddies, I hoisted my large trunk containing all my earthly possessions onto the back of Uncle Albert's rusty truck. Destination: unknown.

Well, not immediately.

Before reaching his home, Albert made a pit stop at the Impala Hotel for a "quick pint." His definition of quick was wildly optimistic. What should have been a five-minute drink turned into a three-hour endurance test, during which I sat sweltering in the truck's cabin like a turkey roasting in an oven.

Eventually, he stumbled back into the vehicle, reeking of alcohol and poor decision-making. Zigzagging through traffic, he somehow managed to steer us into the driveway of his house, a rundown shack in a neglected corner of the city.

My new home.

Albert hauled my trunk out of the truck and led me inside to what I could only describe as a glorified dog kennel. No bed, just a foam mattress dumped on the floor, a pile of mismatched blankets, and an overpowering stench that hit me like a punch to the gut. No wardrobe, no shelves, nowhere to store my clothes, just chaos. A stark contrast to the structure and order of a boarding school.

Things couldn't possibly get worse.

Or so I thought.

At that moment, I seriously considered making a beeline for the Nels' residence and leaving this appalling squalor behind. But, being the ever-optimist (or fool, depending on perspective), I decided to wait for the right opportunity.

It didn't take long to realise that meals in Albert's household were as unpredictable as his sobriety. Breakfast, lunch, and dinner operated on a lottery system; if you were lucky, you'd get something edible. If not, you made do with whatever creative concoction the old drunk cobbled together.

Sausage wrapped in dry bread. Peanut butter and maple syrup… on bread. And the ever-glorious delicacy, corned beef slapped onto a piece of (you guessed it) bread.

Bread. So much bread. And mugs of black tea to wash it all down.

Meanwhile, Albert's diet consisted of a single, unchanging item: beer. Beer for breakfast, beer for lunch, and if beer wasn't available? That's where I came in.

"Go to the bottle shop and get me beer for breakfast," he would bellow. "I don't have money with me, but you pay, and I'll pay you back."

Of course, paying back was a foreign concept to him. Unlike my schoolmates, who at least had the decency to return borrowed money with interest, Albert operated on a strict take-and-never-return policy.

By then, I had accumulated a decent stash of money, enough to book myself into a hotel and escape this misery. But I bide my time, waiting for the right moment. There was just one minor problem: I was still legally a minor. Running away meant risking arrest or worse, being dragged back to this living nightmare.

But there was hope.

Next month was my birthday, my eighteenth. The day I would finally be free.

And then, Albert could buy his own damn beer.

What could go wrong?

***

An Unexpected Conscription Call.

Just when I thought I was on the verge of freedom, I woke up on my 18th birthday to a letter waiting for me:

"Congratulations! You are now eligible for mandatory military service!"

Fantastic.

Suddenly, the horrors of Uncle Albert's bread-and-beer diet seemed like a luxury compared to what lay ahead. I had spent months dreaming about escaping his rundown shack, only to find myself shipped off to boot camp instead. At least at Albert's, I had some level of autonomy (even if it involved running beer errands). Now, a drill sergeant was screaming in my face at 4 AM, and instead of black tea and stale bread, I was eating military rations that somehow tasted worse.

The only consolation? I had gone from planning an escape from a rundown house to planning an escape from military service. Now, instead of sneaking out of Uncle Albert's driveway, I was figuring out how to fake an injury or, at the very least, get stationed somewhere that didn't involve actual combat.

But the ultimate irony?

I ended up liking it.

After weeks of gruelling hell, I realised… I was actually kind of thriving. A structured routine, proper meals (even if bland), and most importantly, an actual bed. Things I never got at Albert's place. Sure, I had to do endless drills and take orders, but at least no one was barking at me to run to the bottle shop at sunrise.

Moral of the Story?

You wanted freedom. You got drafted. And now, Albert's the one laughing, sitting on the porch drinking beer.

So yeah, things could go spectacularly wrong.

***

During the 1970s, South Africa enforced compulsory military service for white males as part of the apartheid government's military strategy. Managed by the South African Defence Force (SADF), this system played a key role in the South African Border War (1966–1989), particularly in South West Africa (now Namibia). Conscripts were deployed in operations against the South West Africa People's Organisation (SWAPO) and other resistance movements, as the government sought to maintain control over the territory despite increasing opposition and international pressure.

The conscription process began at age 16 with mandatory registration, followed by a formal call-up at 18. Conscripts underwent medical and psychological assessments before being assigned to branches such as infantry, artillery, engineers, or specialised units like the paratroopers. The duration of service ranged from nine to 24 months, after which conscripts were placed in the Citizen Force, requiring them to attend periodic refresher training camps for several years. Many were deployed to the Angolan-Namibian border, where they conducted patrols, ambushes, and counter-insurgency operations in harsh conditions, facing extreme heat, landmines, and guerrilla attacks.

Basic training, lasting three to six months, was held at military bases such as Voortrekkerhoogte in Pretoria and the Infantry School in Bloemfontein. Training included weapons handling, endurance exercises, counter-insurgency tactics, survival skills, and first aid. Additionally, there was strong political indoctrination, reinforcing the apartheid government's anti-communist ideology. The training aimed to prepare conscripts not only for combat but also to align them ideologically with the government's military objectives.

Upon completion of training, conscripts were assigned to various branches of the SADF, including elite infantry battalions like the 32 Battalion and 61 Mechanised Battalion Group. Some joined specialised units such as Koevoet, a counter-insurgency and reconnaissance force, while others served in support roles. The nature of their assignments determined their war experiences, with many conscripts exposed to the brutality of guerrilla warfare and the psychological toll of prolonged conflict.

The impact of conscription extended beyond the battlefield, affecting both individual soldiers and South African society. Many conscripts returned with psychological trauma, struggling with post-war reintegration and the lack of recognition for their experiences. Over time, opposition to conscription grew, leading some to flee the country or resist service. As anti-apartheid movements gained strength and international pressure mounted, the conscription system weakened, contributing to the eventual end of apartheid and South Africa's withdrawal from Namibia in 1990.

***

It was a Monday morning, early enough that even the sun seemed reluctant to show its face. With nothing but a wallet, a corned beef sandwich, and a head full of uncertainty, I walked into town and boarded a bus to Pretoria. My destination? Voortrekkerhoogte army camp, where whatever I knew about life was about to be stripped away and replaced with something far harsher.

The moment we arrived, there was no fanfare, no warm welcome, just a battered army truck, its dull green paint peeling under the relentless sun. It wasn't there for a scenic tour. It was there to haul me and a fresh batch of clueless recruits straight into the unknown.

As soon as we climbed aboard, the reality of military life hit like a gut punch.

The induction was a relentless blur of days bleeding into each other, measured not by hours but by shouted orders, punishing drills, and muscles that burned with exhaustion. Our names? Irrelevant. We were reduced to numbers, stripped of identity, broken down and moulded into obedient soldiers.

There was no easing in, no adjustment period, just a brutal wake-up call at an ungodly hour, followed by physical trials that would have made lesser men weep. Hesitation was punished. Complaints were ignored. Personal struggles? No one gave a damn.

We ran. We crawled. We were introduced to the R1 rifle, machine guns, grenades, and tools that we would soon handle with instinct rather than thought. Civilians no more, we became creatures of discipline, moulded in sweat and sheer willpower.

The outside world? Forgotten.

By the time night fell, exhaustion wasn't just a sensation. It was a state of being. Sleep was a luxury, a fleeting whisper that never lasted long enough.

The barracks echoed with the barked commands of instructors who seemed to exist solely to make our lives hell. The military wasn't interested in who we were before we arrived. It was only interested in what it could turn us into.

Weeks passed in a gruelling haze of drills, weapons training, and formations. My body ached in places I never knew existed, my mind was stretched thin, and yet, I endured. We all did. Not because we had a choice, but because the alternative was unthinkable.

And then, one day, my name was called.

There was no time for questions, no chance to process what was happening. Before I knew it, I was shoved into my new reality: the Mechanised Cavalry.

Tanks. Armoured vehicles. The deafening roar of diesel engines.

Gone was the familiar struggle of my past. Uncle Albert's shack, the restless nights spent scheming for a future, I had left all of that behind. And yet, standing before a massive, armoured beast, its steel-plated exterior glinting under the harsh sun, I couldn't shake the feeling that I had traded one form of captivity for another.

I had escaped one cage, only to be strapped inside a rolling fortress of war, heading straight into the unknown.

And something told me…

The worst was yet to come.

***

The Mechanised Cavalry, also known as the Armoured Corps, was a fast-moving, heavily armed division responsible for battlefield dominance through speed and firepower. Their primary role was engaging enemy forces using Olifant tanks and Ratel Infantry Fighting Vehicles in direct combat. They carried out armoured assaults on enemy strongholds, coordinated with infantry and artillery for large-scale operations, and played a key role in cross-border raids into Angola, targeting guerrilla bases. Their ability to rapidly deploy and sustain heavy firepower made them a critical force in South Africa's counterinsurgency efforts.

Another major responsibility of the Mechanised Cavalry was conducting reconnaissance and border patrols along the Angola-Namibia border. They were tasked with locating enemy guerrilla camps, disrupting supply lines, and gathering intelligence on enemy troop movements. Patrolling vast and dangerous territories, they were the eyes and ears of the South African Defence Force (SADF), ensuring enemy infiltration was prevented and that the SADF high command had up-to-date intelligence on threats in the region.

In addition to frontline combat, they provided convoy escort and route clearance, protecting vital supply lines from landmine attacks, ambushes, and Rocket Propelled Grenade fire. Using Buffel mine-protected vehicles and Casspir armoured personnel carriers, they transported troops safely and ensured roads were cleared of explosives. Engineering teams deployed with the cavalry also used armoured bulldozers to remove obstacles and detonate landmines, reducing the risk of casualties during transport and logistical operations.

With their speed, tactical mobility, and rapid reaction capabilities, the Mechanised Cavalry was a key force in counter-insurgency warfare. They were the first responders to enemy ambushes, reinforced threatened positions, and used hit-and-run tactics to outmanoeuvre guerrilla forces. Supporting airborne units and paratroopers, they provided mobile firepower when needed. Their armoured strength and relentless mobility made them an indispensable component of South Africa's military operations, ensuring swift, decisive action in one of the most intense theatres of war.

***

In the early seventies, we were driven to Pretoria Airport, boarded a Hercules C-130 transport plane, and flew north to Windhoek, the administrative centre of South West Africa. From there, we embarked on a gruelling twelve-hour road trip across harsh, dusty terrain, finally reaching Katima Mulilo Base, deep in the Caprivi Strip, where the war was at its fiercest. Nestled near the Zambezi River and bordering Zambia, the base was a frequent target of SWAPO guerrilla attacks, with mortar shells and small-arms fire keeping us on constant edge. The journey itself was a stark introduction to the realities of war, remote landscapes, oppressive heat, and the ever-present tension of an unseen enemy.

During the South African Border War, the South African Defence Force maintained a vast network of military bases across South West Africa to support counter-insurgency operations. Grootfontein served as the primary logistics hub, Otavi housed mechanised infantry, and Windhoek operated as the SADF's regional headquarters. Further north, Oshakati and Ondangwa were crucial operational bases near the Angola border, with Ruacana being a launch point for cross-border raids by 32 Battalion, one of the most feared units of the war. In the east, the Caprivi Strip and Kavango region had key bases such as Rundu, overseeing river patrols, and Katima Mulilo, where we were stationed, closely monitoring SWAPO infiltration routes from Zambia. These bases played an integral role in securing Namibia's borders, executing mechanised infantry operations, and launching strikes deep into Angola. The days were long, the nights were restless, and the reality of war was impossible to escape, whether in the scorching heat of patrols, the deafening roar of incoming mortar fire, or the quiet tension before the next inevitable skirmish.

***

And then, barely a week after my arrival, disaster struck. It was as if misfortune had packed its bags and followed me since the moment I set foot in this forsaken land. First, a bout of malaria that left me feverish and delirious. Then, a sprained ankle that had me hobbling around like an old man robbed of his prime. And now this, a tragedy born of incompetence and the reckless arrogance of our platoon leader.

Serving in the Mechanised Cavalry meant one thing above all else: I was a driver of heavy-duty vehicles. That particular day, my orders were clear: fetch the tow truck and set out to recover a disabled Olifant tank. Simple enough. A short trip, they said. Routine, they assured me. With five of my comrades aboard and the reassuring presence of an infantry escort, we set off. The road stretched before us, dust rising lazily in the African heat, and for half an hour, nothing stirred but the hum of our engines and the rhythmic crunch of tyres against the dry, unforgiving earth.

The tank recovery itself was uneventful, the hitch secured with military precision. We turned back towards base, our convoy moving steadily, one escort at the rear, another ahead. But war has a way of creeping up on you when you least expect it. Like a viper lying in wait, it struck fast and without mercy.

Gunfire erupted from the dense underbrush, tearing through the air with a fury that sent men scrambling for cover. The ambush was swift, relentless. Bullets whistled past, the air thick with the acrid scent of gunpowder and burning diesel. And then madness.

Out of nowhere, one of the guerrillas, either too brave or too foolish for his own good, flung himself into the cab of my truck. Chaos reigned as I struggled, his hands clutching at my tattered uniform, his breath hot with the stench of desperation and rage. In the frenzied struggle, I lost my footing. The next thing I knew, I was tumbling down, down, over the edge of a steep cliff. The world tilted, the sky spinning above me before I plunged into the murky embrace of a swamp below. Silence swallowed me whole, and darkness claimed my mind.

When I awoke, time had become an abstract thing. Was it hours? Days? My body ached, every limb screaming in protest as I found myself bound to a post beneath the shade of a massive tree. My boots were gone, my bare feet pressed against the cool, damp earth. A sharp pain flared in my left arm, a cruel reminder of the battle I had barely survived. Cuts and bruises covered me; souvenirs of a fight I had no recollection of losing. I should have stayed in the camp's infirmary a little longer, I thought bitterly.

The scene around me was surreal, a cluster of mud huts, their walls cracked and weathered by time. Rusted vehicles, long surrendered to decay, stood like forgotten relics of a bygone era. Women moved with practised grace; their children strapped to their backs as they pounded corn in worn wooden buckets. Life carried on as if I were nothing more than another addition to this war-torn existence. No captors in sight. No comrades. Just me alone, bound, and left to the whims of fate.

A child approached, his wide, curious eyes peering at me as if I were some strange, bedraggled creature washed up from another world. In his tiny hands, he held a rusted condensed milk can, filled with water. He offered it to me without a word, and I accepted with a grateful nod, the cool liquid easing the dryness in my throat. A small mercy in an otherwise merciless world.

And so, I waited. For what, I did not know. My fate was no longer my own.

As night fell, my situation changed ever so slightly. Someone faceless in the darkness loosened the ropes binding me to the post, only to replace them with chains around my ankles. A bowl of rice was shoved into my hands, and a couple of ragged blankets were tossed over me. The message was clear: tonight, I would sleep under the stars.

Sleep, however, proved to be an elusive luxury. The ground beneath me was unyielding, every jutting pebble and crooked contour pressing into my back like nature's own cruel joke. The night air was thick with humidity and the constant whine of mosquitoes, who feasted upon me with the enthusiasm of long-lost relatives at a buffet. I lay there, eyes wide in the darkness, as the weight of exhaustion pressed hard against my skull, my thoughts spinning, unsettled.

And in that bitter, breathless stillness, a treacherous thought crept into my mind, maybe, just maybe, the miserable conditions of Albert's house back home weren't so bad after all. At least there, I had walls. And a door. And most importantly, mosquito coils.

The following day, to my great relief, I was ushered into an upgraded accommodation: a more luxurious mud hut, if such a phrase could exist without irony. It had compacted earth floors, a small square window that allowed a single shaft of light to paint golden lines across the room, and best of all, a panoramic roof, or rather a gap between the rafters and thatch that gave me an uninterrupted view of the cosmos.

That would be my room for the next couple of days, humble by most standards, but rich in starlight and solitude, and somehow, in its own way, exactly what I needed.

One day, with the first light of dawn creeping through the cracks in the wooden slats, I was led forward, into a large hut, my chains whispering against the dirt floor with each reluctant step. The air inside the hut was thick with sweat, thick with the acrid scent of old wood and burnt tobacco, thick with the kind of silence that spoke louder than words ever could.

Half a dozen soldiers stood around a small wooden table, their uniforms worn and threadbare, their boots caked with the dust of long marches and forgotten battles. Their eyes followed me, dark and unreadable, but I could feel what they did not say. These were not men playing at war. These were men who had long since been swallowed by it. And in that moment, I knew with a certainty that lodged itself deep in my bones, this was no mere detainment.

Fear is a strange thing. It does not announce itself with fanfare. It does not come screaming. No, it seeps in like a slow, creeping tide, filling every crevice of your being, until you are drowning in it. And I was drowning.

I had heard the stories, the whispered warnings traded between comrades over dim lanterns and half-smoked cigarettes. "If you're taken, they will break you," they had said. "They will carve you open until you tell them everything. And when you have nothing left to give, they will still not be done with you."

The thought settled in my gut like a stone. I tried to steel myself, tried to summon the bravery I had always imagined I would have in a moment like this. But courage, I learned, is a fleeting thing when the future ahead of you is painted in the colours of pain and death.

I was seated across from the table, my wrists raw from the iron shackles, the air so thick with unspoken tension that I could almost taste it. Then, the door creaked open.

The man who stepped inside did not need an introduction. Power clung to him like the heavy air before a storm. He was tall, broad-shouldered, the dark fabric of his uniform pressed to rigid perfection. A smattering of medals adorned his chest, catching what little light filtered through the cracks, glinting like cold stars against the blackness of space. But it was his eyes, sharp, calculating, wholly devoid of warmth, that told me everything I needed to know.

This was a man who did not ask questions out of curiosity. He asked them because he already knew the answers.

The interrogation began, precise and methodical, like the rhythm of a well-rehearsed drill. Name. Rank. Unit. The words were barked more than spoken, clipped and impersonal. I answered, because to hesitate was to invite suspicion, and suspicion was a thing best avoided in rooms like these.

But with each word that left my lips, realisation slithered through me like a slow-moving poison.

I was a Portuguese national, conscripted into the South African army. Fighting in Angola, a Portuguese colony.

A foreigner. A traitor.

The weight of that truth pressed down on me, heavier than the chains around my wrists. In the eyes of Portugal, I was not a prisoner of war. I was something far worse.

The punishment for men like me did not come with trials or negotiations. It did not come with last words or second chances.

At best, I would be locked away in some forgotten prison, the keys tossed into a river, my name erased from existence.

At worst?

At worst, death would come before the sun had set. And if I were lucky, if fortune had not entirely abandoned me, it would be quick.

But looking into the eyes of the man before me, I knew better than to hope for luck.

***

Back at the base, the weight of failure settled like an evening fog, thick and inescapable. The casualties of the botched operation began to mount; each name etched in the ledger of the fallen like echoes of regret. Out of eighteen souls who had set forth into the fray, five would never return. Their journey had ended in the unforgiving embrace of war, their final moments known only to the silent night and the gunfire that had sealed their fate.

Twelve men limped back through the gates, their bodies battered, their spirits heavier than their packs. Some carried wounds visible to the eye, torn flesh, bruised ribs, a limp that would never fully heal. But it was the wounds unseen, the ones that burrowed deep into the marrow of a man's soul, that would haunt them the most. And then there was one unaccounted for. One man, lost to the darkness.

Perhaps he had perished alone, his body lying somewhere beyond the ridges and riverbeds that marked the border. Or perhaps, though none dared say it aloud, he had been taken. A prisoner. A pawn in a game played by men in suits, far from the blood and the dirt. No one knew for certain, and uncertainty is a crueller fate than death.

The following morning, before the sun had fully claimed the horizon, a rescue party assembled. They were volunteers, men who knew the risks, who understood that the odds were thin as a whisper in the wind, but who still shouldered their rifles and laced their boots because a brother left behind was a sin they could not abide. With grim resolve and rifles slung over weary shoulders, they set off, disappearing into the wild unknown, swallowed by jungle and shadow.

Days passed. Then a week. Then two. They searched every ravine, every abandoned hut, chasing every whisper of a lead with the quiet desperation of men who had seen too much and lost too many. Under the veil of night, they crossed the border, slipping past enemy patrols like ghosts drifting through the underbrush. They followed trails that led to nothing but dust and silence, questioned villagers who kept their eyes fixed on the ground, unwilling or perhaps unable to speak of what they knew.

In the end, their search proved as fruitless as a desert in drought.

By the time they returned to base, their heads hung low, not from exhaustion, though they were exhausted beyond words, but from the shame of coming back empty-handed. There would be no triumphant rescue, no cheers in the barracks, no soldier lifted from the jaws of captivity to the warm embrace of home. There would be no tale of heroism to soften the ache in their chests. Only the long, hollow march back through the gates, past the once-lively mess halls, past the faded murals and weary flags, and into a silence that wrapped around them like mourning cloth.

The war, as it always does, had taken another piece of them.

And war, as it always does, never gives back what it steals.

And so, Second Lieutenant Gabriel Duarte Almeida was officially listed as MIA, Missing in Action.

No next of kin. Not dead. Not alive. Just gone, a name in a ledger, a shadow in memory, a question without an answer.

***

The interrogation was brief, efficient, devoid of theatrics, yet brimming with unspoken intensity. A man of considerable stature sat before me, his uniform adorned with ribbons and medals that gleamed under the dim light of the room. I would later come to know that this was no ordinary officer but General Pedro Tonha "Pedalé," one of the highest-ranking figures in FAPLA, the People's Armed Forces for the Liberation of Angola. At the time, I had no inkling of his prominence. I was simply a man caught in a web far larger than himself.

What did surprise me, however, was the civility with which I was treated. No snarling threats, no backhanded slaps across the face. The soldiers moved with a quiet discipline; a calculated restraint that unsettled me more than outright aggression would have. Perhaps they had realised I was valuable, an asset, a bargaining chip. Or maybe they were just well-trained men, indifferent to my fate beyond orders issued from higher up. Either way, they did not mistreat me.

Dressed in fresh civilian clothes, a dark green shirt neatly tucked into matching trousers, I was escorted to a desolate airstrip where a twin-engine Cessna stood waiting, its propellers humming a slow, methodical rhythm. Flanking me were four towering guerrillas, their oversized forms almost comical in their silence. Each held an AK-47, resting between their knees, their fingers absentmindedly drumming against the metal. Not a word was spoken. Not a glance exchanged. It was as if they were statues, moulded by war and hardened by time.

I sat in the back of the plane, a spectator in my own abduction. Through the sweeping view of the cockpit, I could see the pilot and the captain murmuring in hushed tones, their conversation a puzzle I had neither the patience nor the ability to decipher. For the first time since my capture, a wild thought flickered in my mind: what if this plane never made it off the ground? What if it simply nosedived on take-off, a fiery end to my uncertainty? And then, just as quickly, I dismissed it. Survival was the only currency I had left, and I intended to hoard it for as long as possible.

We landed in Luanda under the cover of night. The moment the wheels kissed the tarmac, a blindfold was thrown over my eyes, plunging me into a world of darkness and uncertainty. I was bundled into a vehicle, its tyres rolling across the uneven streets of Angola's capital for what felt like an eternity. We stopped frequently, doors opening, voices rising and falling in hurried exchanges, then shutting again before the journey resumed. I listened, trying to catch anything familiar, but the words slipped past me like water through clenched fingers.

As dawn began its slow crawl across the sky, my captors finally brought me to a halt. The blindfold was yanked away, and I found myself at the foot of an imposing staircase, hundreds of steps ascending toward an unknown fate. My legs burned as I climbed, my breath shallow, my mind racing. At the top, I was ushered into what could only be described as a luxury hotel room. The bed was large, the linens crisp. A far cry from the dirt floors and cold nights I had endured. The door clicked shut behind me, locked from the outside.

For the first time in nearly a year, I sank into the mattress and allowed sleep to take me without a fight.

Days bled into weeks. My only visitors were silent observers, men and women in varying attire, some clad in military fatigues, others in expertly tailored pinstripe suits with brilliant white shirts and colourful ties. They did not speak, did not introduce themselves. They simply looked me up and down, as though assessing livestock at a market, before departing without a word. There was no sign of the general, no clue as to why I was here, only the knowledge that I was being watched, studied, evaluated. Later, I would come to understand that these visits were not random. They were the quiet deliberations of an international diplomatic committee, threading a delicate needle between war and negotiation.

And then, one afternoon, the door burst open. The hotel housekeeper, a woman with an air of practised efficiency, strode in with a purpose.

"Get into the bathroom and scrub yourself clean," she instructed, thrusting a bag of toiletries into my hands. "You will be receiving an important visitor. You need to look presentable."

With no other option, I obeyed. When I returned, she was waiting, scissors in hand. "Sit down," she ordered. "I need to cut your hair and trim that mess of a beard."

By the time she was done, a dark suit, a crisp white shirt, a neatly knotted tie, and polished shoes were laid out before me. Once dressed, I barely recognised the man in the mirror. I had been transformed into one more clean-cut silhouette among the diplomatic elite. And strangely, it felt good. The fabric was smooth, tailored, dignified, nothing like the stiff, scratchy suits my mother had sewn for me a quarter of a century ago, stitched with love but worn like sandpaper.

That evening, I was escorted to the hotel's lavish sitting room, where a man awaited me. He introduced himself as Sérgio Vieira de Mello, a United Nations official. Beside him sat an attractive American woman, her expression unreadable. It was only years later that I learned the significance of that moment.

***

Sérgio Vieira de Mello was a Brazilian diplomat who dedicated his life to humanitarian work, serving the United Nations for over three decades. Born in 1948 in Rio de Janeiro, he studied philosophy at the Sorbonne in Paris before joining the UN in 1969. His early career saw him working in crisis zones such as Bangladesh, Sudan, and Cyprus, where he developed a deep understanding of conflict resolution and humanitarian aid. Over the years, he became a key figure in international diplomacy, advocating for human rights and peacebuilding efforts in some of the world's most dangerous regions.

Vieira de Mello played a crucial role in several high-profile UN missions, including those in Cambodia, Bosnia, and Timor-Leste, where he helped lead the country's transition to independence. He was widely respected for his pragmatic approach, charisma, and ability to mediate between opposing factions. In 2002, he was appointed as the UN High Commissioner for Human Rights, further solidifying his reputation as a global leader in humanitarian affairs. His work often placed him in perilous situations, but he remained committed to his mission, believing in the power of dialogue and diplomacy to resolve conflicts.

Tragically, Vieira de Mello was killed in the 2003 bombing of the UN headquarters in Baghdad, Iraq, where he was serving as the UN Special Representative. His death was a profound loss to the international community, as he was seen as a future Secretary-General of the UN. His legacy lives on through the Sérgio Vieira de Mello Foundation and the annual UN Human Rights Prize named in his honour, inspiring future generations of diplomats and humanitarian workers.

***

"We are going to send you back to South Africa," Sérgio said, his voice smooth as polished stone, his Portuguese flawless. There was something unsettling about his calmness, something that gnawed at the edges of my already frayed nerves.

I stared at him, my mind wading through the thick fog of fear and exhaustion. This was too easy. Too clean. Men like me didn't just get sent back. There was always a price, always another shoe waiting to drop.

Sérgio watched me with the unnerving calm of a man who'd already mapped out every possible move like a grandmaster observing the final moments of a chess game he knew he'd won. His eyes were steady, unreadable.

Calculated.

Then, with a slowness that made the silence unbearable, he leaned back in his chair and said, almost casually, "There is one condition."

Of course there is, I thought bitterly. There's always a condition.

He rose from his seat, the room shifting with him. The soldiers lining the walls didn't move, but their eyes followed silent shadows waiting on cue. Sérgio's movements were deliberate, theatrical even, like a man stepping into the final act of a well-rehearsed performance. He paused, letting the moment stretch, before turning to face me again.

"You're going to pretend none of this ever happened."

A chill settled over me.

His hand found my shoulder, light, almost paternal.

Too gentle. Too controlled.

A gesture that might have been reassurance… if it hadn't felt so rehearsed.

I couldn't tell if it was comfort or a warning.

Maybe it was both.

I frowned, my mind racing. "So, you're saying I was never conscripted? Never captured?"

"Precisely," he nodded, his expression unwavering. "For the past four months, you have been living at Albert's place, looking for work. That is your story. Do you understand?"

I hesitated, the weight of his words pressing down on me. The weeks of captivity had blurred my sense of time, distorted my grip on reality. My mind searched for the catch, the hidden trap, but the pieces refused to align. Was this mercy? A test? A game with stakes I couldn't yet comprehend?

Still, I nodded because that was the only thing to do.

And then, in a moment as sharp as the edge of a knife, it hit me.

Sérgio knew.

Not just my name, not just my rank. He knew more about me than I had ever anticipated. My past. My movements. My connections. Albert's name, spoken with the ease of a man who had done his homework.

I had been stripped, interrogated, broken down to my barest self, and yet, it seemed, they had known all along.

A chill crawled up my spine.

This wasn't a negotiation.

It was a script.

And I was already playing my part.

Sérgio's assistant handed me a brand-new passport and outlined my new life. A commercial flight to Johannesburg, and a driver waiting to take me to the Impala Hotel. A job at the National Bank, where I supposedly had an account. It was surreal, a sudden shift from prisoner to civilian, from forgotten soldier to a man with a fabricated past.

When I finally checked my bank balance, I was met with yet another surprise: ten thousand Rand had mysteriously appeared in my account. A parting gift, perhaps? Or hush money? Whatever the case, I was on the road to financial freedom.

As for Albert, the man whose house I had supposedly called home, he had vanished. No farewells. No explanation. When I asked around, someone muttered he had died. But there was no proof. No obituary.

No grave. Just silence. It was as if he had been quietly erased, like a smudge wiped clean from the margins of a forgotten page.

And so, I stepped out into the world not as a survivor, but as a ghost. A man who had endured the unthinkable, yet in the eyes of bureaucracy and memory, had never existed at all.

Chapter 12:
The Hand that Moved the Pieces.

Jacobus "Kobus" Malan was a formidable Afrikaner in his sixties, a man whose presence commanded both respect and a degree of unease. A former detective and agent of BOSS, South Africa's notorious Bureau of State Security, he had spent his early career navigating the dangerous world of intelligence, counterespionage, and covert operations. His sharp instincts, ruthless efficiency, and ability to extract information by any means necessary had made him both feared and respected. Though the political landscape shifted, Kobus remained a survivor, adapting to the new order with calculated precision.

After retiring from law enforcement, Kobus transitioned into the corporate world, leveraging his connections and strategic mind to secure a position in finance. He had risen to become the Managing Director of the National Bank, overseeing operations with the same discipline and pragmatism that had defined his past. Under his leadership, the bank had thrived, but his approach had remained coldly efficient. He had valued loyalty, discretion, and results above all else. He had understood power better than most, always ensuring he was on the right side of it.

Despite his hardened exterior, Kobus had been a devoted family man, married to a strong, reserved woman who had stood by him through South Africa's turbulent changes. His two daughters, raised in privilege, had distanced themselves from the darker aspects of his past but still recognised his influence. While he had kept his private life tightly guarded, he had enjoyed traditional Afrikaner pastimes such as hunting and whiskey, maintaining a disciplined, methodical routine that had kept him sharp. His network of former operatives, police, and political figures had ensured he remained well-informed in both business and broader affairs.

***

Dressed in my finest attire, freshly pressed, though not nearly as fresh as it had been two days before, I stepped forward, pushing open the heavy wooden doors of the bank precisely at 9:00 AM. The brass handles were cool against my palms, the scent of polished wood and paper thick in the air as I crossed the threshold into a world of quiet efficiency and hushed transactions.

I approached the teller, a young woman with dark hair neatly pinned back, her features bright and professional, yet not without warmth. There was something in her expression, a flicker of recognition, a knowing smile as she glanced up at me.

"We've been expecting you, Gabriel," she said, her voice smooth, practised.

That caught me off guard. Expecting me? I wasn't sure if that was a good thing or something that should set off alarm bells in my head. Before I could ponder it too much, she stepped out from behind her cubicle, gesturing for me to follow.

I trailed behind her through the bank's corridors, my eyes taking in the structured chaos of tellers handling transactions, managers overseeing with a watchful eye, the occasional customer clutching paperwork with the weariness of a man about to negotiate with fate. Then, we stopped outside an office, a space that exuded quiet authority.

The waiting area, however, was a different story. The chair they directed me to, a bucket-style upholstered in an unapologetic lime-green Dralon fabric, seemed like a test of sorts. It was the kind of colour that made statements. Loud ones. As I sank into it, my nerves stirred.

The office itself had walls of rich timber and frosted glass panels, the kind that hinted at power while maintaining just enough mystery to make you wonder what went on behind them. My eyes drifted to the lettering on the door:

Jacobus Malan, General Manager

The sign was bold, authoritative, printed in the no-nonsense Arial Black font, the same font, I noted with some amusement, that had graced the door of my old school principal's office. That realisation sent a shiver of nostalgia mixed with mild dread down my spine. Memories of standing outside that very different door, heart pounding, waiting for judgment, came rushing back.

Before I could dwell on it further, the door swung open.

Jacobus Malan stood before me, a man whose handshake could have cracked walnuts. He carried himself with the confidence of someone who had seen and heard it all, the kind of man who could spot nonsense from a mile away and had no patience for it.

We talked small talk at first, the polite back-and-forth of introductions and pleasantries. Yet, beneath it, I could feel something else. A weight. The distinct, unsettling sensation that he already knew far more about me than I had ever intended to reveal. It wasn't what he said, but how he said it, the slight pauses, the knowing glances, the way he studied me with that measured gaze.

After a few icebreakers, he leaned back in his chair, lacing his fingers together. "I'll call Ms Clark," he said, his voice steady, businesslike. "She'll show you the ropes."

Then he paused, his eyes narrowing slightly as he added, "She's been with the bank for years. If there's anything you need, you talk to her."

There it was again, that feeling. Like I was being carefully placed on a chessboard, my moves anticipated before I even made them.

I nodded, doing my best to look composed, but deep down, I knew one thing for certain.

This was only the beginning.

Ms Clark had been at the National Bank for so long, some whispered she came with the foundations part of the original construction, like the marble floors or the humming fluorescent lights. At fifty, she had devoted her life to managing Mr Kobus Malan's office with the precision of a seasoned field marshal. If efficiency had a face, it would have been hers: unreadable, unwavering, and immune to nonsense. She had never married, and when asked why, she would arch one cool eyebrow and reply, "I have a job, four cats, and bridge on Saturdays. What more does a woman need?"

Her private life mirrored the structure of her professional one, neat, measured, and immaculately uneventful. She lived with her elderly mother, a woman equally committed to silence, symmetry, and the gentle tyranny of routine. Their home was ruled by four cats, each of whom Ms Clark treated like minor aristocrats, their whims indulged with the same diligence she applied to annual reports.

Travel held no appeal. In her view, crossing city limits was a reckless indulgence. "Why suffer the indignity of airports," she once said, "when you can enjoy a properly trimmed hedge and a civilised glass of cherry liqueur?" Her true escape was her garden—a kingdom where the flowers obeyed her without question, unlike the humans at work.

On weekends, she convened with her bridge club, the only arena where she allowed herself competition. She played with deadly focus, once noting with a sly smirk, "Bridge is just like banking, everyone's bluffing, and someone always ends up broke."

Though she kept to herself, Ms Clark knew everything that happened at the bank. She heard, saw, and remembered details with terrifying accuracy, making her the true power behind the throne. She never questioned Malan's decisions aloud, but she had a particular way of pursing her lips that suggested she could, if she wanted to, bring the entire institution crumbling down with nothing but a well-placed sigh. Anyone foolish enough to underestimate her quickly learned that behind her quiet demeanour lurked a mind as sharp as her pruning shears and just as deadly.

Ms Clark led me into her office, a modest but well-organised space adjoining Kobus Malan's suite. The room had the familiar scent of polished wood and old paper, the kind of smell that clung to the walls of institutions where paperwork was king, and decisions were made with the stroke of a pen.

We sat opposite each other, a large table between us, neatly stacked with orderly piles of documents, each sheet, I suspected, holding some bureaucratic secret known only to those who had mastered the art of corporate navigation. Ms Clark exhaled softly, a small sigh of routine, and then offered a smile, revealing teeth so perfectly aligned they could have been modelled in a dental textbook.

"You'll be assigned to the mailroom," she began, her voice carrying the practised authority of someone who had done this a hundred times before. "You'll be assisting Jock. He's retiring at the end of the year."

She paused, tilting her head slightly, "Tea?"

I blinked, caught off guard. No one had ever offered me tea before. Not in a place like this. Not with such effortless kindness.

I nodded, grateful.

With the precision of someone who had poured thousands of cups before, she filled a delicate porcelain China teacup and slid it gently across the table. It was warm in my hands, and for a fleeting moment, it felt as though I had stepped into a different kind of world, one where people exchanged pleasantries over tea, not barked commands or urgent demands.

As I took a cautious sip, she launched into a careful explanation of what the job entailed. It was straightforward, almost absurdly so.

My main duty? Collecting the mail from the mailroom and zigzagging through the office, distributing letters and documents to their intended recipients. That was it.

I sat there, nodding along, but in the back of my mind, a question loomed.

Someone got paid for this?

I had spent years being drilled in discipline, survival, and strategy, yet here I was, being introduced to a system where the most pressing challenge seemed to be making sure a memo reached the right desk. The simplicity of it almost made me laugh. Almost.

Nonetheless, I wasn't about to question it aloud. A job was a job, and I knew better than to take an opportunity for granted.

By late morning, my duties officially began. Jock, a stout man with greying hair and an easy demeanour, trailed behind me, overseeing my first round through the labyrinthine office. The place sprawled across three floors, packed with employees who barely looked up as I passed, too absorbed in their work, their typewriters clattering like a chorus of mechanical insects.

At some point, before I was fully handed over to Jock's guidance, Ms Clark, with her no-nonsense demeanour and an air of quiet authority, led me into the Human Resources office.

It was a stark room, all polished surfaces and the faint smell of ink and paperwork, the kind of place where futures were quietly signed away in triplicate. I was presented with a stack of documents so thick it could have doubled as a doorstop. My head spun before I had even read the first line, but Ms Clark, ever efficient, tapped the first page with her neatly manicured finger, signalling where my signature was needed.

I signed.

And then I signed again. And again. My name scrawled across so many lines that for a brief moment, I half-expected to hand over my soul in the process. With each flick of the pen, I was binding myself to something I didn't fully understand. The words on the pages blurred into legal jargon, clauses upon clauses of obligations I was too young and too eager to question.

But one detail stood out.

One number.

My wage.

I stared at it, my heart stumbling over itself. It was more than reasonable, almost suspiciously so. How was it that pushing a trolley around an office, delivering envelopes and interdepartmental memos, could pay this well?

The realisation settled in quickly, like a shadow creeping across my mind.

This wasn't luck. This wasn't coincidence.

Sérgio.

I had no proof, no signed affidavit linking his name to the numbers on that sheet. But deep in my gut, I knew. His fingerprints were all over this unexpected generosity, tucked neatly between the lines of corporate bureaucracy.

And that thought, more than anything, made me pause.

Was this an act of mercy? Some silent, unseen attempt to right the wrongs of the past? Or was it yet another chapter in a script I hadn't realised I was following, a game being played just beyond my comprehension?

I pushed the thought aside.

And so, my adventure at The National Bank began.

A kid barely eighteen, fresh-faced and untested, stepping into a world I never imagined would have a place for me. A job. A salary. And, more astonishingly, a bank account in my name. There were mornings I had to pinch myself just to be sure it wasn't some elaborate dream.

By then, I had lost touch with my parents, my family, a severance that came not with a bang, but with the slow erosion of hope. I had written letters, each one a thread cast across a widening gulf. I made the calls, waited through the rings, held my breath through the silence. But no one reached back. And so, little by little, the past slipped from my grasp like footprints at low tide, washed clean, leaving only the memory of where they'd once been.

But life, in its own peculiar way, has a method of filling the void.

At the bank, I found something I hadn't realised I needed. A different kind of family.

People who looked out for me, who shared a laugh over coffee breaks and made sure I never felt like an outsider. There was camaraderie in the simplest of moments, the passing of an inside joke, the quiet nod of recognition in a crowded elevator, the way we all somehow carried the weight of the workday together.

It wasn't the family I had lost. But it was something.

And for a boy who had spent years feeling like he belonged nowhere, it was enough.

***

In the late 1970s, a bank trading room linked to the stock exchange was a fast-paced, high-energy environment where traders executed deals through direct phone communication with brokers on the exchange floor. These rooms were large, open spaces filled with desks, rotary-dial telephones, and ticker tape machines, creating a constant buzz of activity. Traders relied on telex machines for international transactions and manually updated stock price boards, ensuring that real-time information was always available. The trading room's connection to the stock exchange was primarily through voice orders and written trade slips, making efficiency and quick decision-making crucial.

Technology in the trading room was a mix of analogue and early digital systems. Rotary phones with multiple lines allowed traders to communicate instantly with brokers, while telex machines provided international market data. Ticker tape machines continuously printed out stock prices, and some advanced banks had early computer terminals such as Reuters or Telerate, offering real-time stock quotes. However, most record-keeping was still paper-based, with clerks manually processing trades and updating chalkboards displaying market movements.

The key players in the trading room included equity traders, bond traders, foreign exchange dealers, and market analysts. Equities traders focused on stocks, while fixed-income traders handled government and corporate bonds. Foreign exchange traders managed currency deals, ensuring that international clients could capitalise on currency fluctuations. Market analysts provided insights on trends, guiding traders in making informed decisions. Clerks and runners played a crucial role in maintaining the flow of trade slips and updates, keeping the entire system running smoothly.

Since electronic trading was not yet widespread, trades were executed through the open outcry system at the stock exchange. Brokers physically present on the exchange floor would receive orders over the phone, signalling trades through hand gestures and loud verbal commands. This meant that personal relationships and trust between bank traders and floor brokers were essential. The reliance on human interaction made the market highly dynamic, where quick thinking and strong intuition played a significant role in successful trading.

The atmosphere of a 1970s trading room was intense and high-stakes, characterised by a sense of urgency and adrenaline-fueled decision-making. Traders shouted across desks, phones rang constantly, and market news could shift financial strategies in seconds. Unlike today's digital trading systems, where transactions are executed with the click of a button, this era of trading relied on human expertise, trust, and rapid communication. It was a time when the stock market was still deeply personal, and those who thrived in the trading room were skilled negotiators, risk-takers, and experts at reading both numbers and people.

***

As I made my daily rounds distributing mail, my attention was increasingly drawn to a small yet intriguing department, the Trading Room. Unlike the quiet hum of the other offices, this space buzzed with energy, staffed by a dozen employees, their eyes glued to monitors, their hands gripping telephone receivers as they spoke in hurried tones. The constant movement, the flashes of numbers on the screens, and the urgency in their voices made it feel like an entirely different world, one that existed outside the routine of traditional banking.

One afternoon, as I lingered a little longer than usual, captivated by the controlled chaos, the symphony of shouting voices, flickering screens, and darting eyes, a sharp-suited trader finally took notice. "You curious about what we actually do here?" he asked, his tone brisk but not unkind. He was in his early thirties, confident, magnetic, the kind of man who moved through the world like it owed him something. Before I could answer, he motioned for me to follow, already turning on his heel. "Come on. I'll show you the heartbeat of the place."

He introduced himself as Gert Wessels, a seasoned veteran of the bank, someone who had spent years navigating the financial markets. What he showed me left me flabbergasted, money changing hands at the speed of light, stocks rising and falling within moments, fortunes being made and lost in the blink of an eye.

People were making money simply by buying and selling shares, not through backbreaking labour, not through endless hours at a desk, but by understanding the pulse of the market. If they could do it, why couldn't I?

The idea took root.

A few days later, with my mind made up, I withdrew one hundred Rand from my account and sought out Gert once more.

"Please buy shares for me," I said, pushing the money toward him.

He smiled, perhaps amused by my determination, but without hesitation, he set up my trading account.

And just like that, I was on my way to becoming a stock market investor.

Over the next year, my investment soared to unexpected heights, thanks to Gert's sharp instincts and the calculated wisdom with which he handled my money. What had started as an impulse decision soon became a new obsession, one that would shape my financial future in ways I had never imagined.

I wasn't just delivering mail anymore.

I was learning how money moved. And I was determined to be part of it.

***

It seemed that whenever I came into contact with money, I had a way of turning it around, a natural instinct that had followed me since childhood. What had started with lending a few cents to my school buddies had grown into something far greater, and now, standing at the edge of a new world, I felt that same familiar thrill of opportunity.

A month after my initial meeting with Gert, he stopped me in the canteen, just as I was about to dig into my Impala Hotel lunch pack, a modest mix of sandwiches and fruit salad.

"Got a minute?" he asked, pulling up a chair across from me.

I nodded, bracing myself, assuming the worst. My shares must have taken a hit.

But then he smiled.

"The shares I bought for you are doing extremely well," he said.

Relief washed over me, a smile creeping onto my face. Losing one hundred Rand in those days would have been catastrophic, and now here was Gert, telling me I had done the opposite.

"You've doubled your money in just a few weeks," he continued.

I grinned, barely able to contain my excitement. But Gert wasn't finished.

"There's something else you should do," he added, pausing as if to let the moment settle. "Some homework."

Ah! Of course. There was always a catch.

Pushing a copy of The Financial Times toward me, he continued, "You should study the stock market. This is the best guide. Check the share movements, make notes," he paused, his tone almost conspiratorial, "If you spot a company that's doing well, point it out to me… and I'll do the rest."

That night, I retreated to the sanctuary of my hotel room, the Financial Times in one hand, a notebook in the other. I pored over the pages, absorbing the rise and fall of numbers, trying to decode the patterns of success and failure.

By the next morning, I had an idea.

As I made my rounds, I cornered Gert, my excitement barely contained.

"The National Bank is doing really well in the market," I said, as if I had uncovered some groundbreaking secret. "I want to take my money and buy shares in the bank."

Gert chuckled, shaking his head. "You already own shares in The National Bank," he pointed out.

I blinked, taken aback. Of course. It was part of the basket he had originally purchased for me. But if I already owned some, why not own more?

Without hesitation, I withdrew another one hundred Rand and bought more shares.

At barely twenty years old, I wanted to buy the bank.

This was just the beginning.

And the best part?

I had all the time in the world.

***

One day, as I was making my usual rounds, weaving through desks and dropping off memos with the efficiency of a seasoned messenger, Kobus Malan's voice cut through the usual office hum.

"Gabriel, step into my office."

My heart dropped like a stone. Had I messed up? Was this the moment my luck finally ran dry?

I quickly unzipped my grey overalls, folding them over my arm like a soldier about to face a tribunal. With measured steps, I entered his office, already bracing for whatever reprimand awaited me.

Kobus sat behind his large mahogany desk, his fingers steepled in thought. His expression wasn't one of anger, nor of disapproval. It was something else, something unreadable.

"Are you enjoying your job?" he asked, his tone almost... polite.

I exhaled, just slightly. "Yes, sir. Very much. And I'm truly grateful for the opportunity."

He nodded, seemingly pleased. Then, after a pause, he asked, "Do you know what a repossession is?"

I frowned, caught off guard by the shift in conversation. Repossession?

I shook my head, half-expecting a long-winded lecture on banking regulations or, worse, some indirect way of telling me I had screwed something up.

Kobus leaned back in his chair and began explaining. He spoke of contracts and unpaid debts, of defaulted loans and the cold inevitability of repossession. But as his words spilled forward, my mind wandered to something entirely different.

Hadn't I, too, been in the business of lending once? Back in school, I had loaned out my pocket money to so-called "friends," only to be met with excuses when the time came for repayment. If only I had the same leverage as a bank, if only I had known I could just take something back when people failed me. Then, Kobus's tone shifted.

"There's a small house, not far from here, that the bank has recently repossessed." He paused, as if weighing my reaction. I nodded, unsure where this was going.

"You could take over the payments," he said simply.

I blinked, my mind stalling like an old engine refusing to turn over.

Was he... was he offering me a house?

I stared at him, puzzled, a giant question mark practically hovering above my head.

"You can afford the payments," he continued, his voice steady, matter-of-fact. "You have a bank account with sufficient funds in it."

That made me sit up.

Sufficient funds?

I knew what was in my account. Or, at least, I thought I did. But the way he said it, the certainty in his voice made something tighten in my chest.

Kobus watched me carefully, allowing his words to settle, to sink in like an anchor on the ocean floor. My thoughts raced: Where had this money come from? And then, like a slow-burning fuse finally reaching its charge, it hit me.

Sérgio.

I had no doubt about it now. This was him. His plan. His doing.

But why? What was the game being played here?

Kobus leaned forward slightly; his expression unreadable. "Think about it, Gabriel. Let me know one way or another."

I nodded, though my mind was still reeling.

Just as I was about to stand, he added, almost as an afterthought, "Oh, there's just one other thing."

I froze.

Of course. There was always a catch.

"There's a car in the garage," he said, a small smirk playing at the edges of his lips. "That's also part of the deal."

I stared at him, trying to process the sheer absurdity of it all.

At twenty years old, I had gone from being a nameless recruit in a foreign land to an office mail clerk with a mysteriously fat bank account, a house, and now... a car?

I wasn't sure if I had stumbled into the greatest stroke of luck in my life or if I was unwittingly being led into something much, much deeper.

And for the first time, I wondered whether I was still playing the role of a free man? Or was I merely another piece in a game whose rules had been decided long before I even stepped onto the board?

***

Imagine stepping into a classic 1960s-style coffee shop, where the air hums with the warm scent of freshly brewed coffee and buttery pie crusts. The walls are adorned with retro pastel hues, mint green, baby pink, and soft yellow, complemented by chrome-trimmed counters and cozy vinyl booths in cherry red.

In one corner, a gleaming jukebox glows with neon lights, spinning rock 'n' roll hits from Elvis Presley, The Supremes, and Buddy Holly. A gentle hum of chatter fills the air as school friends gather at their favourite booth, laughter mingling with the clinking of milkshake glasses.

Behind the counter, a cheerful waitress in a polka-dot dress and a crisp apron balances a tray with tall, frosty milkshakes, their whipped cream peaks crowned with maraschino cherries. Chocolate, vanilla, and strawberry shakes are served in frosted metal cups, alongside steaming mugs of rich coffee poured into thick ceramic mugs.

The pies are legendary golden, flaky crusts filled with warm apple-cinnamon, tart cherry, and rich, creamy chocolate silk. The scent alone draws people in, but the first bite is sweet, buttery, and perfectly spiced, keeping them coming back.

As the bell above the door jingled, another group of students spilled into Nico's Café, their laughter warm against the quiet hum of the sleepy town. Without hesitation, they slid into their usual booth, the one where friendships were cemented over shared milkshakes, where dreams were whispered between bites of hot toast, where the weight of the outside world melted away, if only until the jukebox played their favourite song.

That was Nico's, the heart of the High Street, the town's unofficial meeting place. Right across from the one and only cinema, it stood as a beacon for restless teenagers looking for a place to belong. It was our place, the one where we gathered before we were deemed old enough, brave enough, or reckless enough to venture into the Impala Hotel's Gold Bar.

Every Tuesday at five sharp, we would meet there, our routine as predictable as the sun setting behind the hills. From Nico's, we'd make the short walk to Hanna's, the town's beloved bowling alley, where victories were celebrated, defeats exaggerated, and the sound of rolling pins filled the space between our conversations.

And then came Saturday afternoons when the smell of buttered popcorn drifted from the cinema doors, and we found ourselves back at Nico's, waiting for the lights to dim and the big screen to transport us somewhere far beyond the limits of our small town.

But that week, something was different.

I was restless, eager, the kind of eager that makes time stretch unbearably slow, where every second drags its feet, teasing you with the weight of an impending decision. Kobus had made me an offer. A proposal that could change everything. And I needed to know what my friends thought.

So instead of heading to Hanna's for our usual bowling ritual, I steered the conversation elsewhere. We needed to talk. I wanted their

opinions, their insights, their gut reactions. *Should I accept Kobus'
offer? Should I let myself take over the house payments?*

It wasn't just about the money. It was about what it meant. About
pride. About freedom. About a future I was still trying to piece
together.

And so, at barely twenty-one, I found myself seeking wisdom from the
only people I had ever truly trusted, my old school friends. They were
my age, some barely a year older, fumbling through adulthood just as
blindly as I was. But I had no mentors, no father figure, no seasoned
guide to show me the ropes. All I had were these brothers-in-arms,
boys turned men too soon, whose laughter had once echoed through
the dormitories and whose loyalty had never wavered. In their flawed,
unpolished way, they were the only role models I had.

The twins were the first to arrive, sliding into the booth with easy
familiarity. Then came Candice, her sharp eyes already reading my
mood before I even spoke, followed by Monica, still adjusting the belt
of her gown. She had just taken over The Wave, the little hair salon on
the High Street, and the smell of freshly washed hair and styling
products clung to her like a badge of success.

We waited.

Glenn stumbled into the café soon after, his mobility struggles still
visible but never slowing him down. And lastly, Hendrik, polished,
sharp, somehow transformed into a proper salesman at the
Volkswagen dealership. The same Hendrik who once lent me his
school notes now wore a suit like he had been born for it.

We gathered around the table, milkshakes in hand, the air buzzing with
a familiar camaraderie. The diner lights cast a warm glow over us,
reflecting off the chrome edges of the table and the half-melted shakes
sweating in their glasses. Outside, the night hummed with distant
traffic and the occasional burst of laughter from passersby, but in that
moment, the world was just us, this table, this conversation, this
decision.

I laid out my situation, speaking slowly at first, then with growing conviction. My good fortune, my dilemma. The weight of possibility and the fear of making the wrong choice. The silence that followed was thick with consideration, but not judgment. These were the people who had always been my sounding board, my gut check, the ones who would tell me the truth even when I didn't want to hear it. I searched their faces, looking for a reaction, a flicker of agreement or concern.

And then, we voted. Hands rose without hesitation, a few with knowing smirks, others with quiet, encouraging nods. The result was overwhelming. My heart thudded against my ribs as I counted them, part of me braced for resistance that never came.

No one questioned whether I could do it, only whether I was ready, and in that moment, I knew I was.

My new home, or rather, not so new, rested beneath the gentle canopy of jacaranda trees lining Sheba Street, their blossoms cascading like violet confetti onto the cracked pavement below. An imposing stone retaining wall stood sentry, weathered but proud, the same wall I had only glimpsed in passing the day before. Yet somehow, it felt right. There was a quiet recognition in its bones, a whisper of belonging I couldn't quite place, as if the house had been waiting for me all along.

It was decided.

A simple thing, really, a vote, a conversation, a few raised hands. But to me, it felt monumental, like stepping through an invisible door I could never return through. The air around me seemed to shift, lightened somehow, charged with the quiet energy of something just beginning.

I grinned, the adrenaline of certainty rushing through me. The path ahead was unpaved, uncertain, but for the first time in years, maybe decades, I wasn't afraid of it. And now, I couldn't wait to tell Kobus. He had always believed in me, sometimes more than I believed in myself. I wanted to see his reaction, to hear his voice when I told him I was taking over the repossession. My future, uncertain, unpredictable, and entirely my own, was about to begin. Whatever came next, success, failure, struggle, triumph, it would be on my terms. And that, more than anything, was what I had been searching for all along.

The following day, I rushed over to the bank, my feet hardly touching the ground. The morning air was crisp, but I barely noticed it. My pulse raced with anticipation; each step fuelled by the decision that had taken root deep inside me. By the time I reached Ms Clark's desk, I was huffing and puffing, my excitement nearly impossible to contain. She looked up from her paperwork, raising an amused eyebrow, but before she could ask, I flashed her a grin and motioned toward Kobus' office.

Moments later, I found myself sitting across from him, fidgeting as he engaged in a long telephone call with what was clearly a difficult client. His tone was calm but firm, his fingers drumming lightly on the desk in that way he always did when dealing with someone particularly stubborn. Every few minutes, he gestured for me to be patient, and I tried truly, I did, but my heart pounded against my ribs, my leg bouncing with unrestrained energy. The words I wanted to say pressed against the back of my throat, demanding to be spoken.

Finally, he hung up the phone. I barely waited a beat before leaning forward, the words spilling out in a rush. "I've decided I'm taking over the repossession!" The declaration felt electric, as if speaking it aloud made it even more real. My chest swelled with the weight of the moment, my hands gripping the armrests of the chair as I waited for his reaction.

Kobus didn't blink. He didn't gasp, didn't lean back in shock, or ask if I was sure. Instead, he simply gave me that knowing look, the one that said he had expected this all along. A slow smile tugged at the corner of his mouth, his fingers steepling beneath his chin as he regarded me.

"Of course, you are," he finally said, nodding as if this had been the only outcome possible. And in that moment, I realised maybe it had been.

***

Two days later, I summoned my old schoolmates to see the inside of my new house for the first time. To me, it was nothing short of a palace: solid walls, a roof that mostly held, and a front door that didn't need a crowbar to open. But to them, it was more of a haunted relic, a crumbling time capsule that hadn't seen human life in years. The windows were streaked with grime, the floorboards creaked like they were whispering secrets, and out back, a sun-bleached Fiat sat slouched in a corrugated iron shed, rusting gracefully into the earth like it had given up on ever being driven again.

The key turned with a soft click, and I pushed the gate open, stepping once more beneath the jacarandas. Their lavender petals drifted around us like confetti, a quiet celebration of something old becoming new again. Beside me, Hendrik said nothing, just gave me a nod, that solid, knowing nod as if to say: *You've come full circle.*

The stone path curved gently toward the porch, and I took my time. The house stood patiently, modest, weathered, real. It didn't sparkle. It didn't need to.

Inside, the scent of mould and dust hit like a wave. Furniture lay under heavy white sheets, and the windows wore faded curtains, some hanging lopsided, a few panes cracked or missing entirely. The silence wasn't empty, it was waiting. This wasn't a retreat, but a return.

Candice, ever the optimist, stepped in, clapped her hands, and grinned. "Well," she said, "what a golden opportunity to tidy this place up and throw a party when it's done."

We laughed, not the kind of laugh that fills a room, but the kind that mends something quietly inside, and for the first time in a very long time, I didn't feel like a guest in my own story. I felt like a man, finally truly home.

The days that followed unfolded in a rhythm both unfamiliar and deeply comforting. There were no deadlines, no ticking clocks, just paint cans, elbow grease, and the laughter of friends who had known me long before the suits, before the headlines, before the loss.

We worked side by side, Hendrik, on the roof, muttering about structural integrity while perched like a mountain goat; Candice orchestrating the interior like a stage production, brandishing swatches and colour samples with theatrical flair; Glenn in the garden, sleeves rolled up, claiming dominion over weeds as if they were misbehaving balance sheets.

And Monica, ever resourceful, toiled behind an old sewing machine in the front room. She'd raided Patel's shop earlier that morning and returned triumphantly with armfuls of fabric in wild, abstract patterns. By nightfall, the house was slowly coming alive not just with light and colour, but with the unmistakable feeling of being *lived in* again.

Someone found a radio in a cupboard. We dusted it off, tuned it to a crackling old station, and let it play while we worked jazz, gospel, the occasional golden oldie that pulled a smile from somewhere deep.

Windows were repaired. Floorboards sanded. The old Fiat was hauled into the sun, its rusted frame now a running joke between us all, "Gabriel's second retirement plan," Glenn would quip, patting its hood with mock affection.

We scrubbed, fixed, patched, and laughed, not always easily, but freely. With every corner cleaned, every wall repainted, something inside me shifted.

The house was no longer haunted by what had been lost. It was becoming something new, not a museum of memory, but a home for what could still be built.

That evening, as dusk draped Sheba Street in lavender hues and the last of the jacaranda petals drifted to rest like memories on the breeze, we gathered beneath the trees for a humble meal. Nothing elaborate, just torn bread, marinated olives, charred meat from a smoky braai, and the kind of laughter that hums beneath the surface, quiet but soul-deep.

One of the twins unearthed an old guitar, the other a weathered ukulele, and together they strummed out Beatles tunes in a lopsided harmony that somehow made the music even more endearing. Before long, we joined the impromptu jam, our voices rising with the chorus of "Let It Be," shaky but full of heart.

Someone lit candles in old jam jars, their flickering flames casting gold across our faces. Wine flowed into mismatched glasses, some chipped, some cloudy, and we sat in a loose circle, basking in the gentle communion of it all. The air was thick with rosemary and roasted garlic, conversation weaving between us like a hymn, low and sacred. It was the kind of night that didn't need to be remembered to be unforgettable.

I looked around at their faces, weathered, kind, familiar and felt something I hadn't in a long time. Not just gratitude. Not just peace.

It was joy.

Not the kind that blazes in headlines or shines from stages but the quiet, steady kind that comes from knowing you're exactly where you're meant to be.

And as the stars blinked awake above the trees, I leaned back in my chair, the sounds of home all around me, and let it all settle into my bones.

I was here.

I was whole.

I was home.

Chapter 13:
Ledgers and Fate.

In the 1970s, banks operated primarily through physical branches, with most transactions requiring in-person visits. Banking hours were typically limited to weekdays from 9 AM to 3 PM, leading to long lines, especially on Fridays before the weekend. The use of Automated Teller Machines (ATMs) was still in its early stages, so cash withdrawals, check deposits, and other transactions had to be handled by a teller. Without digital records, banking was slower, relying heavily on paper-based ledgers and filing systems to track customer accounts and transactions. Monthly bank statements were mailed, and customers had to balance their chequebooks manually.

Checks were a primary method of payment, and clearing them took several days due to manual processing through clearinghouses. Loans and mortgages were handled through face-to-face meetings, requiring extensive paperwork and a personal relationship with the bank. Credit history was verified through references rather than digital databases. While credit cards existed, they were not as widely accepted, making cash the dominant form of daily transactions. Wire transfers were costly and slow, limiting the ability to quickly move funds between banks.

Security relied on traditional measures such as signature verification, vaults, and armed guards, with fraud detection being largely manual; similarly, counterfeit bills were a concern, but tellers relied on experience to identify them. Meanwhile, early banking technology, including large mainframe computers, was introduced in some institutions but was primarily used for back-office operations rather than direct customer service. In addition, the introduction of MICR (Magnetic Ink Character Recognition) technology helped speed up check processing, but automation was still in its infancy.

Despite these limitations, banks emphasised customer relationships, often knowing their clients personally and making lending decisions based on trust and financial history rather than just numerical credit scores. Banking was highly regulated, and competition between institutions was limited. The 1970s set the stage for significant changes in the following decades, including deregulation, the expansion of ATMs, and the shift toward digital banking, ultimately transforming how people accessed and managed their money.

***

My career at the bank was going from strength to strength, or at least from mildly confused to vaguely competent. I was learning new work practices, building relationships, and for the first time in a long while, I felt like I was part of something bigger than myself.

Everyone seemed intent on helping me along, offering advice, passing tips, occasionally patting me on the back as if to check I was real. I soaked up every bit of knowledge like a sponge, albeit the kind of sponge that occasionally leaked under pressure.

Eight months after I first stumbled into mail distribution, Ms Clark summoned me to her office.

I stood hesitating at the door, half-expecting to be told I had accidentally mailed someone's mortgage papers to the janitor again. Stepping cautiously inside, I sat down opposite her desk, wearing the kind of hopeful grimace usually reserved for people about to receive dental news.

She gestured to the chair with the solemnity of a judge passing sentence. "We have decided," she said, steepling her fingers, "to assign you a more responsible position."

My heart did a small, clumsy somersault. Promotions! Responsibility! Power! Also, terror!

Ms Clark explained that a staff member had been promoted to another branch, leaving a crucial void. The timing, she admitted, wasn't perfect, which was a polite way of saying "this might end in flames," but the position had to be filled immediately.

She slid a cellophane folder across the desk. Inside was a neat sheet of bullet points, listing my new responsibilities with all the thrill of a microwave manual.

Forty-five minutes later, I was deposited into the Ledger Department, now under the wary command of Mr. van der Merwe, a man who looked as if he had been professionally disappointed by life since the reign of Queen Victoria.

Wrinkled, short, and permanently infused with the faint scent of burnt coffee, Mr. van der Merwe was a monument to methodical routine. His idea of living dangerously probably involved adding a fourth sugar to his tea.

He led me to my desk with the enthusiasm of a man escorting livestock to a slow-moving abattoir.

"You receive the cheques," he said, deadpan. "You write them in the ledger. Name. Payee. Amount." He paused dramatically, as if revealing ancient banking secrets.

"And don't," he added, narrowing his eyes, "make the columns wonky."

Simple enough, I thought. Boring, mind-numbing, sure. But manageable. Except that's not how it turned out.

Thanks to my old schoolmate Glenn, who had once taught me his tricks for photographic memory in between stuffing his face with toffee, I began absorbing account details like a supercomputer crossed with a nosy neighbour.

Within a year, I knew everyone's accounts by heart. Their bank balances. Their spending habits. Their guilty little payments to suspiciously named "consulting" firms.

At first, it was harmless, just a parlour trick in the ledger labyrinth. But soon, the whispers began. "Hey, Gabriel," someone would mutter, glancing around nervously. "Mr Oosthuizen wants to cash a cheque. Has he got the funds?"

I'd flick through my mind like a card catalogue and answer without hesitation. "Yep," or sometimes, "Better not, unless he's planning on robbing a few vending machines."

Word spread. Faster than a rumour at an office party.

Soon, even senior staff started treating me like some sort of financial oracle. I became the human shortcut to the filing cabinets faster than a computer, more accurate than a calculator, and (according to one cheeky teller) "a lot easier on the eyes than the ledger department's mouldy wallpaper."

My memory, once a quiet, slightly embarrassing party trick, had turned me into something valuable. Respected. Consulted. Sometimes, even brought coffee, no strings attached.

And while the days blurred into a steady rhythm of numbers, ledger entries, and quiet nods of recognition, another side project quietly flourished.

My little share portfolio, quietly, obsessively nurtured in secret, was my rebellion in a pinstripe disguise. Each stock, a whispered act of defiance, each dividend a silent victory no one saw coming.

And in the stillness of the late hours, those quiet stretches when Barberton slept, and the city hummed like a resting giant, I would lie awake, staring at the ceiling, letting myself imagine the impossible:

One day, I would own the National Bank.

Not working at the National Bank, but owning it.

It wasn't a plan exactly, more like a shimmering dream, soft around the edges but sharpening with every late-night calculation, every successful little investment.

It felt good.

Too good.

And then just as I allowed the thought to settle, to nestle warmly into my bones came the voice.

Quiet. Persistent. A whisper curling through my mind like cigarette smoke.

What could go wrong?

Because if life had taught me anything, it was this: Just when everything feels certain, life will reach out with both hands and shake the very foundation you thought was unshakable.

And it never did so gently.

***

Cornelious Anton Swart was a man whose presence commanded attention. Towering and broad, his bald head and clean-shaven face gave him an air of no-nonsense authority. He was always dressed in his signature brown safari suit, carrying the weight of his past as a former South African police officer in his rigid posture and disciplined demeanour. His deep, commanding voice demanded respect, and when he spoke, people instinctively listened.

As the Marketing Director at the head office, Cornelious applied his tactical mindset to the corporate world, treating business negotiations like high-stakes operations. He was a man of results, intolerant of inefficiency and unimpressed by excuses. His reputation preceded him, respected by those who worked with him, feared by those who fell short of his expectations. His methods were tough but undeniably effective, making him a driving force in his field.

A heavy smoker, the scent of tobacco lingered around him, a subtle reminder of long nights spent strategising. Despite his gruff exterior, there was a sharp intelligence behind his eyes, a mind that calculated every move before making it. Cornelious was not just a man of authority; he was a man of presence, one who left a lasting impression wherever he went.

***

I had just turned twenty-four when, once again, I was summoned to Ms Clark's office. But this time, unlike before, I wasn't the least bit nervous.

155

By now, I had built a solid reputation at the bank. My work was meticulous, my relationships with colleagues were strong, and I carried myself with the kind of quiet confidence that comes from knowing you're doing well.

So, when I bounced into Ms Clark's office, I half-expected to be greeted with a cup of tea and a digestive biscuit, the usual small comforts she offered during our chats. Settling into one of the visitor chairs, I flashed an easy smile, waiting for whatever news she had to share.

After a brief bit of small talk, she got to the point.

"The Marketing Director from Head Office will be travelling up to meet with you," she announced.

My easy smiled faded, the room tilted, breath hitched, and every nerve in my body went cold.

I hated unexpected news. It rattled me in a way few things could. Why would someone from Head Office be coming all this way just to see me? And then, the real fear set in.

What if this had nothing to do with my work? What if they had discovered something?

My mind raced to the past I had buried. My escape from Angola. The way I had slipped away, the past I had left behind. I had worked so hard to rebuild my life here to become someone new, someone safe.

And now, for the first time in years, I felt that life was teetering on the edge.

For the next few nights, sleep was a stranger. I lay awake, my mind spiralling through worst-case scenarios. Was this meeting about my immigration status? Had someone uncovered a detail I thought was long forgotten? Could this be the moment where everything unravelled, where I'd be forced to run again?

By the time I returned home from work that evening, the weight of uncertainty was crushing me. I had to talk to someone.

I found Glenn, now one of my "repossessed home" housemates and told him everything Ms Clark's announcement, my fears, the meeting that loomed over me like a storm cloud.

He listened patiently, arms crossed, his usual sharp gaze unreadable. And then, with the certainty of someone who had known me too long to entertain my paranoia, he said, "You're overreacting."

Maybe he was right. Maybe this was…to unfold, but deep down, I couldn't shake the feeling that something was coming.

And whatever it was, I had to be ready.

Three days later, I stepped into the bright, sunlit boardroom, where coffee and cakes were elegantly arranged on the highly polished table. The aroma of freshly brewed espresso mixed with the scent of varnished wood, and beyond the floor-to-ceiling windows, the manicured courtyard stretched out in perfect, peaceful symmetry.

It felt surreal, too refined, too orchestrated for a simple meeting.

At the far end of the room, Cornelius Swart stood, offering a firm handshake, his grip warm, his expression open. As I studied his body language, a sense of relief settled over me. He was genuinely pleased to meet me. This wasn't an interrogation. This wasn't a reckoning. This was something else entirely.

Introductions out of the way, he turned toward a flip chart, its pages filled with diagrams, columns, and figures, reminiscent of an economics lecture. His voice carried the practised ease of a man accustomed to holding a room's attention.

And then, as the presentation unfolded, I was floored.

The board of directors had made a decision about my future, a future that had been meticulously mapped out, planned in boardrooms and strategy meetings without me even knowing it. My career wasn't just progressing; it had been designed, structured, and propelled forward with a precision I hadn't dared to expect.

What had started as a humble position at the National Bank had now catapulted to unexpected heights. I wasn't just another employee climbing the ladder, I was being fast-tracked, moulded, and positioned for something greater.

It was overwhelming and exhilarating, and for the first time in my life, I wasn't just surviving, I was ascending.

In summary?

I would be sent to university to study economics and marketing, fully sponsored.

My courses would begin at the start of the year.

I would remain at the bank one day a week in my current role because, as Cornelius put it, I was too valuable to let go.

The realisation hit me in waves. Security, growth, and a future. For the first time in my life, I felt as though the ground beneath me was solid.

By the end of the day-long session, I stepped out of the boardroom, reams of documents tucked under my arm, my mind still racing to catch up with the sheer weight of what had just happened.

It felt surreal, like stepping into a future I hadn't even realised was mine.

And then, as I reached for the door, something unexpected happened.

The corridor was lined with familiar faces, my colleagues, my peers, the very people I had worked alongside, laughed with, learned from, and at the head of the endless line, Ms Clark and Kobus Malan with a grin ear to ear.

And then applause.

It started as a ripple, then swelled into a wave, filling the corridor with a sound I never imagined would be for me.

A standing ovation.

I froze for a moment, scanning their faces. There was no envy, no hesitation, only pride, encouragement, and something even more powerful… belief.

They had known before I did.

Gert Wessels greeted me with a grin wide enough to outshine the sun and a pat on the back that nearly knocked the wind out of me; no words were needed; that gesture said it all. And as I stood there, letting the moment sink in, a quiet thought settled deep within me one I had never allowed myself to fully embrace.

Maybe, just maybe, I was exactly where I was meant to be.

***

Fast forward three and a half years.

Graduating with a bachelor's degree in economics and marketing, had felt almost effortless in the end, a smooth conclusion to a journey paved with late nights, relentless studying, and an unshakable determination to carve out a future for myself.

It wasn't just about the degree. It was about everything it represented. The late nights steeped in self-doubt, the sacrifices made quietly, the countless moments of mental and physical exhaustion, where I had questioned if any of it was worth the price. And now, standing there with my diploma in hand, I realised this wasn't just a piece of paper. It was a symbol of survival, of ambition, of proving to myself that I could rise beyond what I was told I would be. I was no longer on the sidelines. I was on the cusp of a new chapter, one that would take me far from everything familiar.

The transition to the Head Office in Cape Town was no longer a distant dream. It was a certainty.

But first, a few years back at base. The bank had offered me a promotion, a new title, Marketing Manager, a strategic stepping stone designed to ease me into the profession, to test the waters before diving into the deep end of Cape Town's fast-paced corporate ocean. I embraced the role, knowing that every campaign, every meeting, every success, and stumble would become part of the foundation I'd stand on when I eventually stepped into the limelight of the head office.

And yet, as my departure date crept closer, I found myself caught in that familiar crosswind of excitement and nostalgia.

On one hand, there was the thrill of the unknown, the undeniable pull of new opportunity, of polished boardrooms and towering office blocks, of high-stakes decisions and the electric hum of a city pulsing with ambition. But on the other hand, there was the quiet ache of what I would be leaving behind the life I had built through sweat and luck and sheer willpower, the friendships that had carried me through the hardest days, the city that had become a kind of home, even with all its imperfections.

Change had arrived full of promise and tinged with the soft sadness of turning a page.

I was teetering on the edge of thirty, standing between past and future, between the comfort of what I knew and the promise of what lay ahead, and for the first time in a long time, I had no idea which side of that line felt more like home.

Before my departure, I wanted to gather my closest friends one last time, to celebrate not just my next chapter, but the journey that had led me here, the struggles, the triumphs, the people who had shaped me along the way.

The house, once a modest and unremarkable space, had slowly transformed into something that truly felt like mine, a reflection of the life I had built, the struggles I had overcome, and the sense of stability I had fought so hard to achieve.

Gone was the old Fiat, that loyal, battered companion that had come bundled with the repossessed home, a banger by every definition, but one that had carried me through the tumultuous early days of my journey. It rattled like a coin tin on gravel roads, coughed defiantly on cold mornings, and yet, it had never let me down. That car had borne witness to countless commutes, quiet insecurities, and the silent hopes of a young man determined to carve out his place in the world. It had taken us on endless escapades to the Swazi Casino, glided (or wheezed) through long, lazy drives across the Makhonjwa Mountains, and served as the background to more stories than I could count.

In its place now stood a sleek Volkswagen, polished to perfection, its engine humming with the quiet confidence of progress. It wasn't just a car, it was a statement, a symbol of transformation. It spoke of how far I'd come without saying a word. It wasn't ostentatious or flashy. No, it was precise, refined, purposeful, a quiet victory on four wheels.

The deal itself was a stroke of fortune, and the credit went entirely to Hendrik, who had somehow, as he often did, charmed his way into the good graces of the dealership's upper ranks. With a few phone calls and a well-timed lunch or two, he'd managed to secure me an excellent discounted sale, a gesture that felt more like a silent toast to everything we'd been through together.

Thanks to him, my transition into the next chapter of life came not only with a sense of direction, but with a smoother, more stylish ride, one that didn't just move forward, but glided forward, with a past in the rearview mirror and possibilities stretching endlessly ahead.

The garden, once overgrown and unkempt, had been reimagined into a beautiful oasis, thanks to Tannie Magda, who had taken it upon herself to coordinate a full makeover. She had directed the workers with the precision of a seasoned architect, overseeing every detail from the lush flowerbeds bursting with colour to the paved pathways that now wound through the greenery. At the heart of the garden stood the BBQ area, its brickwork solid and inviting, a place that had already seen its fair share of late-night laughter and long conversations.

This was where we would say goodbye.

As the sun dipped below the horizon, casting streaks of orange and gold across the sky, my friends began to arrive. The twins, always inseparable, showed up first, carrying a cooler filled with drinks. Candice, ever the organiser, brought homemade snacks, while Monica, fresh from a long day at the salon, arrived still in her work attire but with her signature carefree energy intact. Glenn, always dependable, had come straight from work, his shirt sleeves rolled up, already eyeing the BBQ pit.

By the time Hendrik arrived impeccably dressed, as if he were attending a gala rather than a backyard gathering, the party was in full swing.

The fire crackled, casting warm embers into the night air as we gathered around the BBQ, plates piled high with food, drinks in hand, reliving old memories. We laughed about our school days, about the pranks we had pulled, the heartbreaks we had suffered, the ridiculous dreams we had once believed were out of reach.

And then, as the night deepened, we moved to the fire pit, the flames painting flickering shadows on our faces. Someone started singing softly at first, then louder as others joined in. The songs were old favourites, ones that reminded us of who we had been before life had begun pulling us in different directions.

We danced, we sang, we held onto the moment as if we could freeze time.

By the time the first pale streaks of dawn crept across the horizon, the fire had died down to glowing embers. One by one, my friends began to leave, their hugs lingering just a little longer, their words carrying more weight.

"Don't forget us when you're a bigshot in Cape Town," Glenn teased, clapping me on the back.

"Just don't come back with a fancy accent," Monica joked, wiping a tear before it could fall.

Even Tannie Magda, who had always been more of a guardian than a mere friend, pulled me into a firm embrace. "You've made us proud," she whispered, and for the first time that night, I felt the sting of tears in my own eyes.

Two days later, with my bags packed and my heart heavy, I was driven to Johannesburg Airport. The roads that had once felt so familiar now seemed distant, like the last pages of a book I wasn't quite ready to close.

As I boarded the flight, I turned for one last look at the city stretching beneath the waking sky, a mosaic of memory and dust. The plane banked gently, tracing a wide arc over the Makhonjwa Mountains, and for a brief moment, it was all still there. The streets I had wandered barefoot and broken. The houses with their chipped paint and sunlit windows. The rooms that had once contained my fears, my dreams, my silent prayers. Each corner a chapter, each rooftop a punctuation mark in the story I was leaving behind. I pressed my forehead to the window, watching it all fall away, not with sorrow, but with quiet reverence.

The past, at last, had somewhere to rest.

And then, there were the people, the ones who had stood by me, who had lifted me when I stumbled, who had made the journey worth remembering.

Seconds earlier, as the plane rumbled down the runway and the engines roared to life, I felt the ground slip away beneath me both literally and metaphorically. With that lift, something heavier than gravity let go. A chapter long, tangled, unfinished, finally folded shut in the roar of take-off.

But as we soared higher, cutting through the clouds, I realised something.

I wasn't just leaving.

I was arriving.

Chapter 14:
From Cape Town to the World.

For reasons that still baffle me to this day, just two weeks into my new role in Cape Town, I received an urgent memo from Richard Campbell, the CEO of the bank, summoning me to his office.

When Richard J Campbell sends for you, you don't delay. You run.

That morning was spent poring over the details of an assignment that, at first glance, seemed far too straightforward for the amount of fuss it was receiving: a meeting with Greek business leaders in Athens, regarding issues related to the sizable Greek community in South Africa. In my opinion, the matter could have been resolved with a phone call and a detailed telex. But I said nothing. I was still new, still testing the currents.

Richard was no ordinary CEO. He was a wizkid of corporate banking, three decades deep in asset management and strategic finance, best known for his conservative approach to risk and his almost surgical precision in leadership. He lived in the affluent suburb of Constantia with his wife, Katherine, a former UN advisor, and their two sons. That weekend, I had been invited to his colonial estate after a long, punishing round of golf at the prestigious Steenberg Golf Club. The whole affair felt like a quiet assessment, a test of readiness.

And so, with a mixture of suspicion and ambition, I boarded a South African Airways flight to Athens. I arrived late afternoon at Eleftherios Venizelos Airport, where a driver delivered me to a city hotel. For the next three days, I was locked in lengthy, often circular discussions with so-called "prominent businessmen," who, in a surprising show of appreciation, showered me with gifts and elaborate souvenirs. It was flattering, if not entirely warranted.

On the fourth day, after a quick sightseeing tour of Athens, I was dropped off at the airport for my return journey via Rome to Cape

Town. But shortly after take-off, aboard a TWA flight, the world unravelled.

Two hijackers stormed the aisle. One grabbed a flight attendant and dragged her to the cockpit, the other shouting threats in heavily accented English, pistol raised high. Panic erupted. Passengers ducked, screamed and prayed. The hijackers barked orders and began collecting passports in a large plastic bag, then vanished to the front of the plane.

It was only much later, and without warning, that we realised we had landed in Beirut. The cabin filled with tension as the doors opened. We were joined by half a dozen more armed rebels, dressed in rags, faces half-covered, weapons gleaming under the airport lights.

Chaos followed. The hijackers returned, holding a small stack of passports. Names were read aloud, mostly women and children. Mine was the last name called. My blood ran cold. I thought: *This is it. This is how it ends.*

Blindfolded, wrists bound, we were shoved down the aircraft stairs into an old, battered bus. The air was stiflingly thick with heat and the sharp sting of jet fuel. The ride was fast and chaotic. No one spoke.

We were delivered to a crumbling, bombed-out building. Inside, we were divided into groups of three. I could no longer hear the others. Children were crying. Women shouted in Arabic, oddly comforting, because somewhere in my frayed logic, I believed they wouldn't torture Arab women.

Days passed. Or maybe it was just one long, sunless day that never ended. I was alone in a small concrete room, the smell of dust and decay hanging in the air. My clothes were in rags, water was scarce, and food, scarcer.

Then, one day, the door burst open.

A man, not in uniform, barked at me: "Get out, go!" My heart slammed against my ribs. *Was this it? Was this the execution?*

Outside, the sun was blinding. I staggered forward, blinking against the light, disoriented until I saw it. A white van, its large blue UN letters like a beacon in the dust, idled just beyond the rubble. A fragile promise of escape.

We zigzagged through the battered arteries of Beirut, weaving past charred cars, crumbling facades, and dazed bystanders who looked like they, too, had forgotten what peace sounded like. Hours passed, though it could've been minutes before we pulled up outside a weathered waterfront hotel.

Inside, calm returned in measured steps. A medical team met me at the entrance. They stitched the cut on my scalp with quiet precision, their touch clinical, their eyes kind. Someone handed me a towel. Then came the shower, my first in days. The hot water stung like judgment, washing away blood, grime, and a small piece of whatever armour I had left.

Waiting for me in the room: a crisp black suit and a white shirt, folded with military care. I dressed slowly, my hands still trembling, as if every movement might wake the nightmare I had just escaped.

Within the hour, the driver from the UN van, a man of few words, returned. He handed me my passport, the very same one I'd last seen disappear into the hijackers' plastic bag, along with a plane ticket. Calm and efficient, he escorted me to the airport, guided me through check-in, and walked me to the gate.

Just before I stepped through, he pressed my wallet into my hand, banknotes and credit cards still intact. Then he spoke, his voice low, flat, and final.

"Pretend that this didn't happen. For your own safety."

I nodded, puzzled. And with that last-minute warning echoing in my ears, I walked across the bridge into the aircraft.

No luggage. No souvenirs. Just a body intact, a passport in hand, and a soul still catching up to what had happened.

And then, just as I was boarding, I noticed a man in a white suit standing alone on the distant passenger viewing balcony. He raised a hand in a slow, deliberate wave. I hesitated, then waved back, unsure whether the gesture was meant for me or for someone else entirely.

I returned to Cape Town, quieter, thinner, and changed, though I wasn't ready to admit just how much.

The incident vanished without a trace. No press conference or debriefing. Not even a single question asked. It was as if an invisible hand had reached out and erased my trip to Athens.

***

Never in a million years had I imagined that my relocation to Head Office would come wrapped in such unexpected riches. Oh, I knew there would be opportunities, a larger stage upon which to prove myself, but the sheer scope of the transformation was something else entirely. The directors had placed a bet on me, and I was determined, with every fibre of my being, to prove them right.

With my new role came privileges that once belonged in the realm of distant dreams, an exquisite apartment perched high above the city skyline, where the twinkling lights below reminded me how far I'd come. A sleek company car, its engine a quiet symphony of power and precision. An expense account that, in one swift stroke, erased the days of stretching a paycheck to the very last dime. It was a world I had once observed from the outside, nose pressed against the glass, wondering what it might be like to step in. Now, the doors had swung wide open.

Yet, for all its luxuries, my arrival wasn't just about personal gains; it was about purpose. The Marketing Department was an aging beast, lumbering forward on outdated formulas that had long since lost their bite. The world had changed, but it had not. And so, it became clear that change wasn't just necessary; it was inevitable.

For the first time in my career, I had the rare privilege of shaping a team from the ground up. The power of choice was mine, presented neatly in a stack of résumés that had been discreetly placed on my desk, each one representing a possible piece in the puzzle of reinvention. I studied them carefully, weighing experience against ambition, knowledge against raw, unfiltered hunger. In the end, balance was the answer. A team composed of equal parts wisdom and rebellion, seasoned veterans who carried the institution in their bones, and fresh minds unafraid to challenge the status quo.

Empowerment became my motto. Not control, not micromanagement, but trust the kind that unlocks potential and breathes life into stagnant spaces.

And, oh, did it work.

Brilliantly.

Success came in waves, not as the result of rigid schedules or suffocating hierarchies, but through freedom, flexibility, and a fresh perspective on what work could be. There comes a time in every person's life when they realise that the rigid constraints of a nine-to-five existence are nothing more than relics of an old world, a rhythm imposed, rather than chosen. And when that moment arrives, one has two choices: stay shackled to the past or carve out a new way forward.

I chose the latter.

Gone were the sterile boardrooms and the artificial hum of fluorescent lights, the stifling monotony of pressed suits and measured steps. No longer did I suffer the tyranny of choking ties and shoes designed more for display than for comfort. No, sir. I embraced a new kind of uniform light linen shirts that moved with the breeze, comfortable loafers that whispered instead of clicked against the floor, and the unmistakable aura of a man who dictated his own tempo.

And as for meetings? Well, why should they be held in stiff, air-conditioned boxes when the world itself offered grander, more inspiring settings? Deals were no longer signed in cold conference rooms but over the soft murmur of the tide at the Yacht Club, where the scent of salt and success mingled in the air. Negotiations unfolded on the lush greens of the golf course, where a keen eye for the fairway mirrored the precision needed in business. And when the occasion called for it, we let the rhythmic crash of waves at a beachside restaurant punctuate our conversations, where ideas were exchanged over seafood so fresh it still carried whispers of the ocean.

Something incredible happened along the way. Work stopped feeling like work. Instead, it became a fluid extension of life itself, an organic, ever-evolving process that didn't just happen at a desk but in the spaces where inspiration lived. Conversations became richer, decisions sharper, ideas more audacious. The world, it seemed, had a way of rewarding those who dared to rewrite the rules.

And so, with each passing day, I embraced this new rhythm, a rhythm not dictated by time sheets, outdated policies, or expectations forged in another era, but by something far greater. The simple pursuit of a life well and truly lived.

For the next ten years, we didn't just market a bank, we built an empire. Our campaigns were not mere advertisements; they were declarations. We redefined The National Bank's presence across South Africa, turning it from a financial institution into an undeniable force. The name became woven into the fabric of everyday life, etched into the consciousness of millions. You couldn't escape it. Turn on the television? There we were. Flip through the radio? Our jingles played on repeat, catchy enough to stick in the minds of even the most reluctant listeners. Billboards stood like towering sentinels along highways, our branding so bold, so unmistakable, that even a fleeting glance was enough to imprint it in memory.

We didn't just advertise.

We dominated!

When we launched a new product, it wasn't announced; it was unveiled in the kind of grand fashion reserved for royalty and revolutionaries. The finest hotels, the most exclusive venues, places where chandeliers dripped with opulence and glasses clinked in celebration became the stage for our meticulously curated events. High-profile clients, industry leaders, and investors weren't just invited; they were immersed in an experience, one that whispered of prestige, exclusivity, and power.

The momentum was unstoppable.

This wasn't just about banking anymore. It was about transformation. About making people feel like they were part of something larger than themselves, a financial institution that wasn't just keeping up with the industry but reshaping it. Clients felt it. Employees felt it. Even competitors couldn't deny it.

And the results? Well, they spoke for themselves.

Our client base didn't just grow, it exploded, quadrupling in size, catapulting The National Bank to the undisputed pinnacle of the South African financial sector. Market share surged, profits soared, and the institution that had once been just another name in the industry became the name.

And with that success came the kind of reward that only reveals itself to those bold or stubborn enough to push beyond their limits. I was promoted to Marketing Director, a title that carried more than just responsibility. It carried weight. Respect. Presence. It wasn't handed out casually. It was earned, forged in the fires of late nights, hard lessons, and relentless persistence.

The timing was no coincidence either. The promotion aligned perfectly with the retirement of Cornelious Anton Swart, the very man who had once stood before a flip chart and, with calm certainty, mapped out the future I hadn't yet dared to dream. His departure made way for my arrival, not as a replacement, but as the next chapter in a carefully built legacy.

It was more than a title. It was a seat at the table. The table where decisions were made, where strategies were carved out like battle plans, where futures were shaped, and legacies built, not with noise, but with every word carefully spoken, and every silence purposefully held. I had arrived not by accident, not by inheritance, but through the quiet, relentless climb of someone who once lent coins from a hollow bed frame, who learned the weight of value before he knew the weight of money, and who now sat with a voice that carried across boardrooms overlooking skylines.

And then came the rewards for a job well done. A staff bonus was distributed all around, lifting morale and gratitude like a tide. My own bonus? I poured it, with familiar discipline, into my growing share portfolio, but this time, with a little extra set aside for something more personal.

A shiny silver Porsche. Not for the show. Not for the thrill. But as a quiet monument to my childhood deprivations, to every moment I had walked when others rode, to every time I had pretended not to want what others had.

This wasn't just a car, it was a whisper to the boy I once was:

"We made it."

And for the first time, I allowed myself to truly feel it.

Not just pride. But belonging.

But by then, I was no longer just an executive.

I had built something something powerful, and when wielded wisely, this power comes with its own kind of reward. A substantial share portfolio, one that didn't just reflect success but cemented something far greater.

Ownership.

Not just of a title, or a position, but of a legacy.

***

After months of meticulous preparation, delicate negotiations, and the kind of strategic manoeuvring that happens only at the highest levels, our department achieved what many had thought impossible: we secured the sponsorship of the prestigious South African Open tournament. It was a defining moment, not just for the bank but for all of us who had poured our energy, our expertise, and, at times, even our sanity into making it happen.

When the news was made public, we celebrated as if we had just won a championship ourselves. It wasn't just another corporate deal; it was a milestone, a symbol of the bank's growing influence, a testament to our ability to stand shoulder to shoulder with the giants of the business world. And as it turned out, the Board of Directors believed that such a victory deserved more than just handshakes and congratulatory memos.

As a token of appreciation, they surprised our team of twelve with an all-expenses-paid holiday to Mauritius, partners included. For a group of seasoned professionals who had spent months buried under contracts, proposals, and high-stakes meetings, it was the kind of reward that made the struggle worth it. The thought of trading in boardrooms for beaches, laptops for loungers, and conference calls for cocktails by the sea was almost too good to be true. But as it turned out, Mauritius had more in store for me than just white sands and turquoise waters.

I met Jessie Parker on the eve of a major tournament, at one of those galas where everything felt like a scene from a well-funded dream. The lighting was always forgiving, the champagne endlessly replenished, and people glided rather than walked, rehearsed in the choreography of influence. The room hummed with the quiet confidence of old money and new ambition.

She wasn't just another guest; she was *the* presence. Jessie Parker. A name whispered across courts from Melbourne to Monte Carlo. A high-ranking South African tennis professional with a reputation forged in sweat and sunlight, she moved with a poise that came not from vanity but from years of discipline, pain, and triumph. She wore her success like a perfectly tailored jacket, never ostentatious, always precise.

Jessie moved like a verse in motion, measured, graceful, impossible to ignore. She didn't seek attention; it followed her like a well-trained shadow. Her posture told you she'd never lost an argument with herself. Her eyes were hazel with flecks of gold, held the same steely calm she'd used to dismantle opponents under stadium lights.

Her body bore the signature of a life spent in motion, athletic but feminine, honed by repetition and resilience. Her skin, kissed bronze by the South African sun, gave off a soft glow that cameras dream of and poets envy. Her hair, pulled back in a no-nonsense ponytail, only made her cheekbones sharper, her focus clearer. When she laughed, and she rarely did, it came from deep within, like thunder finding sunlight.

Jessie dressed with a kind of silent rebellion against fashion's louder trends. A crisp white blouse. Tailored trousers. A vintage wristwatch that looked inherited, not purchased. Her style was never about the label. It was about the intention. She was timeless, not trendy. You got the sense she didn't follow the world's tempo; she set her own.

There was something about her I couldn't name at the time. A steadiness beneath the glamour. A quiet magnetism. She wasn't just beautiful, she was grounded. And that made her rare.

Jessie was a woman of the world in the truest sense, someone who had chased sunrises across continents, who had dined in places I'd only read about, trained on clay courts that bordered the Mediterranean, and strolled through European cities like she had left a piece of herself in each one.

What I didn't know then, what no one could've told me, is that Jessie Parker would become more than a dazzling memory from a gala. She would become a force in my life, a turning point wrapped in grace and grit. But that night, under chandeliers and starlight, I simply watched her, unaware that the story had already begun.

Her family, the Parkers, were synonymous with South African winemaking, the custodians of a vast, centuries-old estate in Stellenbosch whose vintages graced tables from London to New York. Mr and Mrs Parker lived amidst quiet luxury, splitting their time between an estate in the South of France and a hilltop villa in the

United States. Their world was one of old vines, old money, and the kind of taste that didn't shout. It simply opened another bottle.

I don't remember the exact moment I fell in love with her; there was no grand revelation, no cinematic thunderclap. It happened slowly, then all at once. In the way she listened without needing to speak, in how she carried herself through rooms without ever needing to prove she belonged. It was in her laughter during long drives, her silence during hard days, and her complete disinterest in being impressed by my titles or success. With Jessie, I wasn't a banker, or a strategist, or a man chasing power. I was just a man, and for the first time in my life, that was enough.

And then there was me. Thirty-two years old, successful in my own right, but embarrassingly untraveled. My world had been business meetings and marketing strategies, a cycle of deadlines and promotions, victories measured in numbers and titles. But Jessie? She looked at the world differently. For the first time, someone made me realise that there was so much more beyond the borders of my own making.

We started dating soon after, and before I knew it, she had me flipping through travel books, poring over photographs of faraway cities and landscapes that seemed almost too surreal to be real. Hours were spent daydreaming over glossy pages, tracing the outlines of places I had never been, yet suddenly longed to see.

And I remember feeling a quiet kind of embarrassment. How had I made it this far in life without ever stepping outside my own country? Without ever feeling the rush of stepping into the unknown, the thrill of navigating unfamiliar streets, the sheer wonder of seeing something for the very first time?

But that was about to change.

Because if there was one thing I had learned from Jessie Parker, it was that the world wasn't something to be observed from a distance. It was something to be touched, tasted, and fully, unapologetically lived.

***

Balancing our schedules was no easy feat. Jessie's life revolved around the relentless cycle of the international tennis circuit, while mine was tethered to the ever-evolving demands of the corporate world. Yet, somehow, we made it work.

She had an apartment in Hampstead, one of those rare London enclaves where time moved like jazz unhurried, textured, deliberate. It was a quiet sanctuary tucked just beyond the chaos, a sunlit corner of the world where the air smelled faintly of old books and lavender, and the city's sharp edges softened into whispers.

It became our refuge. Our lovers' nest. A hidden place stitched into the seams of our busy lives, where the world slowed just long enough for us to exhale. Between tournaments and deadlines, we retreated there to rest, to reconnect, to remember what it felt like to simply *be*.

When our calendars aligned, we'd meet elsewhere too, sometimes in the States, sometimes in the hushed corners of Europe. Grand cities that hummed with history, or nameless little towns where we could walk hand-in-hand through empty squares without turning heads. In those places, unburdened by expectation or applause, we became something rare: two people not performing, just living.

My frequent travels meant that I amassed an almost absurd number of Air Miles, enough, I joked, to circle the globe a dozen times over without spending a dime. And yet, it wasn't just about miles or destinations, for something had shifted inside me. I had become enchanted by the world, as each new place, each foreign street, and each unfamiliar skyline felt like stepping into a different universe.

I was enchanted with travel, yes, but more so with Jessie. She had a way of turning every city into a stage, every detour into a story. With her, airports became gateways to possibility, not just destinations. A missed train in Florence, a storm delay in Vienna, a wrong turn down a cobbled alley in Lisbon, each mishap transformed into a memory, simply because she was beside me.

She made the world feel intimate, as if the universe had shrunk to the size of a hotel room with rumpled sheets and shared laughter. I wasn't just seeing new places, I was seeing them through her eyes, eyes that had already witnessed so much, yet still widened in wonder. And that's what travel became to me: not escape, but arrival. A coming home not to a place, but to a person.

Jessie.

I stood in awe of towering cathedrals that had withstood the test of centuries, marvelled at the solemn beauty of temples where prayers had been whispered for generations. I found myself drawn to different religions, different cultures, and the infinite variety of human expression. Travel had cracked open my mind, revealing a world far greater than boardrooms and bank statements. Every city, every country was an adventure, an unfolding story that I was eager to read.

It was in the early eighties, at a board meeting in London, that my journey took yet another unexpected turn. The room was filled with the weight of power; of men whose decisions shaped the future of the bank. And at the head of the table sat none other than Sir Godfrey Vaughn, the formidable chairman, a man whose mere presence could silence a room.

The meeting proceeded as expected, numbers and projections dominating the conversation until Sir Godfrey shifted his focus to me.

"The board of directors," he began, his voice measured and deliberate, "has considered your relocation to our head office in London."

He paused then, long enough to let the words settle, long enough to watch my reaction.

"You don't have to make a decision right away," he added with a small, knowing smile.

I froze. For a split second, the room around me ceased to exist. The murmurs of executives, the polished mahogany table, the weight of expectation, all of it faded into the periphery, swallowed by the gravity of what had just been said. My mind struggled to grasp it, as if my body had yet to catch up with reality.

I pinched myself. A quiet, almost absurd gesture. A relic of childhood disbelief, the kind of thing a boy does when he wakes from a dream too grand to be his own. But this was real.

And then, as the meeting concluded, something unexpected happened. One by one, the room rose to their feet. Applause filled the air, not the polite, customary kind, but something richer, something that carried weight. Respect. Recognition. Another milestone won. Another battle fought and conquered.

Yet, as I stood there, pride swelling in my chest, something else crept in, a quiet kind of ache, an emptiness that applause could not fill.

I was celebrating this moment alone.

The abandoned boy, the one who had once known the cold indifference of the world, who had learned to fend for himself, who had built his life with his own two hands, had made it. He had stood before giants and had been counted among them. And yet, there was no father's handshake, no mother's embrace, no childhood home where he could return with stories of triumph.

And then, from the depths of my memory, Sérgio's voice surfaced. "You are going to pretend that none of this ever happened."

The words struck like a whisper from the past, unravelling themselves in the silence of my thoughts. What had he meant? Was it a warning? A challenge? A quiet absolution from a man who had seen more than he cared to admit?

Was this life the success, the recognition, the power, a dream I had willed into existence? Or was it the universe's way of balancing the scales, of rewarding a child who had once been left behind? Had Sérgio felt sorry for the abandoned boy, or had he simply seen something in me that I had yet to recognise in myself?

It was a victory, yes. But it was also a reckoning.

Some achievements are celebrated in grand halls. Others, in the silence of the soul.

***

It was late when I returned to The Dorchester Hotel, its timeless grandeur standing in quiet contrast to the whirlwind of thoughts racing through my mind. The doorman tipped his hat, unaware that the man crossing the threshold was no longer quite the same. The lobby, with its marble floors and golden chandeliers, glowed softly as an oasis of calm against the backdrop of a life suddenly thrown into motion.

The crisp London air still clung to me, sharp and bracing, like the news I had just received. I moved through the halls on instinct, barely noticing the soft hush of footsteps on thick carpet, the distant clink of glassware from the bar. My thoughts crackled like static: names, possibilities, consequences. It wasn't just a career shift, it was a seismic pivot, a door swinging open onto a world I wasn't sure I was ready for.

Up in my suite, the city lights shimmered beyond the window, indifferent to the storm within. I poured myself a drink, something aged and expensive and stood there in silence, letting the weight of it all settle. Outside, London pulsed on, but for a moment, time belonged to me.

Without hesitation, I dialled Jessie in Los Angeles.

The line rang only once before she picked up, and the moment I spoke, her excitement was impossible to disguise. Laughter, disbelief, joy, it all tumbled through the receiver, stretching the distance between us into something weightless, insignificant.

For hours, we talked, voices weaving between dreams and reality, laying out the plans for my relocation to London. The decision felt big, monumental, even, but with Jessie on the other end, it also felt right.

When I returned to Cape Town, there was only one thing left to do: celebrate.

I gathered my friends, my true family, for a night in the city, a chance to mark the end of one chapter and the thrilling start of another.

By now, I had quietly financed Candice's dream, a stud farm she had once described with starry eyes and nervous laughter over a shared milkshake. What began as a whimsical notion had grown into an empire. She poured her soul into the land, the bloodlines, the discipline, and soon her name echoed across auction houses and equestrian circles from Europe to the Middle East. Clients flew in from around the globe, chasing the excellence she had so meticulously bred. Millions in sales followed, but it wasn't the numbers that moved me; it was the memory of that first conversation and the quiet pride of knowing I had helped her believe in herself before the world did.

My friends had stood by me through everything.

I never forgot that.

They had been there in the early days, when success was a distant mirage, when my ambitions were no more than ideas scribbled in notebooks. And now, as I stood on the brink of a new life in London, I knew one thing with certainty: I would always help them in return.

Because if it weren't for my half-dozen friends, I wouldn't be here.

I wouldn't have this success, this freedom, this independence.

And no matter where life took me, that was something I would never take for granted.

***

Fast forward eighteen months: my professional and personal life in South Africa had been neatly gift-wrapped, labelled, and left to bake under a merciless thirty-degree sun. Meanwhile, I found myself stepping off a plane and straight into a London winter that could have frozen the soul out of a penguin.

The cold hit me like a disapproving British butler, brisk, brutal, and impeccably dressed. Gone were the days of short sleeves and lazy sunsets; now I was trading in UV rays for sleet and sarcasm. Yet, beneath the layers of thermal shock, there was an undeniable thrill buzzing in my veins: this was the beginning of something new, slightly insane, but gloriously new.

Navigating the arrivals hall with the dazed wobble of a man who had just time-travelled, my eyes locked onto an attractive young woman, waving with the polished enthusiasm of someone about to upsell you a five-star hotel upgrade. She was my welcome committee, complete with a knowing smile and a voice crisp enough to slice cheddar.

"Mr Almeida," she chimed, her accent pure London clipped, cultured, and possibly capable of sending invoices just for speaking.

Reality hit me then: this wasn't a holiday. I wasn't a tourist. I live here now. Good Lord !!!!!

The drive through London's frostbitten streets felt like a guided tour through a Christmas card. Iconic landmarks loomed out of the mist, powdered with snow and glowing softly against the early dusk, like grand old dames dressed up for one last, glorious ball.

Our destination: a temporary residence in Mayfair, the kind of neighbourhood where even the pigeons wear bespoke waistcoats.

The moment I stepped inside, warmth wrapped itself around me like an expensive cashmere hug. The place was understated luxury incarnate, quiet confidence in every detail, from the antique brass doorknobs to the Persian rug that probably had a better education than I did.

Above the roaring gas fireplace hung a massive abstract painting, bold strokes and defiant swirls locked in eternal, chaotic battle. It was the kind of art that either inspired deep contemplation... or gave you a migraine if you stared too long. Either way, it dominated the room like a tipsy uncle at a family wedding.

Through the tall sash windows, Berkeley Square stretched out in pristine, snow-dusted elegance, framed by charming historic buildings that looked as though they'd been plucked straight from a Jane Austen fever dream. It was, frankly, absurdly perfect like living inside a postcard somebody had Photoshopped for maximum whimsy.

I stood there for a long moment, letting the scene settle into my bones. This wasn't a dream. This wasn't a pit stop. This was my new life. Mayfair. London. *Me.*

Just as I was beginning to embrace the stillness, the front door exploded open like a champagne cork, and in stormed Jessie. She charged into the room with the uncontainable energy of a tennis champion, fresh from a Wimbledon victory, radiant, triumphant, practically bouncing off the walls.

"Welcome to London!" she cried, her laughter filling the room like sunlight streaming through storm clouds.

Gone was the winter gloom, gone was the solemn grandeur Jessie had brought summer with her, early delivery. Glasses were found, champagne was uncorked, and once again, we toasted:

To another chapter. To another beginning. To the absurd, thrilling, ridiculous beauty of it all. London had finally arrived.

And, in a slightly more dishevelled but determined state …so had I.

Chapter 15:
For Sérgio.

At precisely 8:00 a.m., not a minute before or after, Bill the chauffeur rang the doorbell with the ceremonious poise of a man summoning royalty to breakfast. I grabbed my winter coat and scuffed briefcase and dashed across the Carrara-marble-floored lobby, my hurried footsteps ricocheting like a badly tuned orchestra warming up for a command performance. Outside, the world had vanished beneath a thick, unbroken quilt of snow. London's overnight transformation into Narnia was impressive, if slightly inconvenient. No fauns, no lamppost magic, just grumpy cabbies, frozen gutters, and the unmistakable swagger of a city that had no idea how to handle weather but insisted on wearing it like couture.

Bill, dressed in military precision and a scowl that could wrinkle glass, opened the door of the Rolls-Royce Silver Shadow, my gloriously over-the-top chariot where the heated seats cradled me like a favoured heir on his way to a coronation. Destination: Paternoster Square, the beating heart of London's financial jungle, where dreams were minted, lost, and occasionally misplaced under a stack of quarterly reports.

At the National Bank's cathedral-like reception, where marble columns stood so stiff you half-expected them to bark at you for scuffing the floor, I was met by Miss Harris, my newly appointed personal assistant.

"Mr Almeida," she said, offering a nod so impeccably timed it could have synchronised with Big Ben. "Welcome to your kingdom."

I followed her through endless corridors lined with cubicle-bound souls, heads bowed to the great god of Spreadsheet, each one greasing the unrelenting gears of this financial behemoth. This place had been my dream once. Now, it smelled of polished wood, ambition, and just the faintest whiff of collective caffeine dependence.

Finally, we stopped before a door so polished I could check my tie in it. There, mounted proudly, was a brushed aluminium nameplate that read:

Gabriel D. Almeida
National Brand Director

New Times Roman font, black, authoritative, the kind of lettering that whispered, "This man signs things."

I stood there a moment, half expecting a heavenly choir to kick in, but all I got was Miss Harris clearing her throat politely.

Inside, the office unfolded like a spread from a Victorian interiors magazine. Dark mahogany desks, antique clocks ticking self-importantly, thick carpets that threatened to devour entire briefcases. It was exactly as I'd envisioned it, a place of gravitas and genteel power curated to the last tassel by the woman now standing crisply at my side.

Ah, yes, Miss Harris.

A quintessential English rose; she bore the serene elegance of someone who could orchestrate a bank merger and bake a perfect Victoria sponge without breaking a sweat. Early forties, polished shoes, perfume like a summer garden at dusk, and an aura that suggested she could outmanoeuvre a parliament of bureaucrats with nothing more than a raised eyebrow.

Born and raised in King's Lynn, where the sheep outnumber the scandals, she had been forged in the iron-clad tradition of rural English pragmatism. Commercial Law degree, with distinction, because, naturally, she approached studying the way most people approach, dodging tax ruthlessly and with the end firmly in mind.

She had turned down shinier jobs in shinier cities, preferring the labyrinthine absurdities of banking where her twin talents, organisational wizardry and discreet savagery, could truly shine.

"Miss Harris," I said, easing into the leather chair behind the mahogany desk with the sort of sigh reserved for weary monarchs and overworked men in new roles, "I trust you've hidden all the bodies left by my predecessor?"

Without so much as a blink, she slid a leather-bound planner across the desk, each tab lined up like disciplined soldiers.

"Of course, Mr Almeida. Filed alphabetically under *Minor Inconveniences.* Shall I forward their ghostly complaints to Accounts, or would Legal prefer to wrestle with the afterlife today?"

I laughed an actual laugh. She didn't. Miss Harris's sense of humour moved like a stealth bomber: silent, elegant, and capable of reducing entire boardrooms to rubble without ever raising her voice.

And there I stood framed by the vast sweep of glass, high above Paternoster Square, staring out at St. Paul's Cathedral, its dome catching the pale winter sun like a monument to resilience itself. Beyond it, the Thames shimmered at the horizon's edge, winding its patient way through the heart of the city.

Over the years that followed, Miss Harris didn't merely manage my life; she fortified it. She became the keystone in the crumbling arch of my ambition, the calm conductor of chaos, and the quiet sentinel guarding my time, reputation, and, on more than one occasion, my dignity. Thus, birthdays were never forgotten, meetings were never missed, and crises were neutralised before they even had the courtesy to knock. Even scandalous rumours were silenced so efficiently, it was as if they'd died of natural causes in their sleep.

And through it all, she moved with that serene, almost ecclesiastical grace, like arranging my life was no more taxing than trimming a bonsai or selecting the correct teaspoon for chamomile.

To the rest of the office, she was a legend spoken of in hushed tones and cautious admiration, a woman said to have once stared down a furious board member until he apologised *to the chair*. But to me, she was something infinitely rarer: a true ally. Wrapped in tweed, armed with surgical sarcasm, and fuelled by tea brewed at thermonuclear strength, she was the constant in my storm.

I stood still, a solitary figure in a suit, high above a bustling world, carrying the silent satisfaction of another dream conquered and the unshakable loneliness that often rode in its shadow.

In that quiet, golden moment, I made a silent vow: never to forget the ones who had bet on me when I was still nothing but rough clay, my schoolmates, my protectors, and, of course, Gert Wessels, my unofficial financial consigliere. Gert, who fielded my midnight calls with weary humour, who bought shares on whispered instructions from a man chasing a future no one else could quite see. Together, we built something extraordinary, one dividend, one risk, one sleepless night at a time.

The bank around me pulsed with relentless energy. My twenty-person team, young, hungry, brilliant, moved at a pace that would have exhausted lesser men. We ran the department like a ship in stormy waters, steady at the helm, quietly ruffling feathers on the executive floor. Some directors wore smiles when they saw me coming; others wore thinly veiled resentment. Success, I learned, was an excellent spotlight but an even better magnifying glass.

For a decade, I crisscrossed the globe like a man chasing the sun: Madrid, Hong Kong, Cape Town, Beijing. Airports blurred into boardrooms; hotel beds blurred into meeting rooms. I kept the old engines running, greased the ancient cogs of international finance, and along the way, paused when I could always in South Africa to find fragments of myself among the faces of old friends, scattered now like dandelion seeds across the world.

And in between all the business meetings, boardroom negotiations, and jet-lagged landings, my school friends were never far from my mind. No matter how far I'd travelled in miles or status, their voices, their laughter, the memory of those formative years remained a quiet constant in the background.

I remember one particular conversation with David Richards, who was in urgent need of someone capable of reengineering the operations behind their high-performance engines, a crucial step in securing Apex

Automotive's entry into Formula One. Without hesitation, Hendrik van Zyl came to mind. Years earlier, I had been instrumental in placing him as head of operations for a South African rally team, where he had proven himself with the kind of grit and precision few could match.

Within a month, Hendrik took up his new role at Apex's Silverstone headquarters, a move that thrilled Richards and reaffirmed what I already knew: the bonds we formed in the dusty courtyards of our boarding school weren't just sentimental. They were real, enduring and, when needed, quietly powerful.

Those friendships were more than memories; they were ballast. In a world where handshakes often came with conditions and praise was sometimes just a prelude to negotiation, the loyalty of my old schoolmates felt pure, unchanging. They didn't care how many shares I held or what title sat under my name. To them, I was still Gabriel, the boy who once bartered chocolate bars for extra bread rolls, who hid savings in a bedframe and plotted the future with ink-stained fingers and stubborn hope. Whenever I reached out, they answered with no delay, no agenda. And in a life that often demanded I wear masks, their friendship was the one place I could be entirely unguarded.

Amid the chaos of boardrooms and balance sheets, my love for Jessie became the one constant I clung to. In a world that demanded everything, she was my pause, my breath, my beginning.

Together, we carved out something rare, a sanctuary hidden from the roar of ambition. We bought a crumbling mansion in The Boltons, a faded relic of London's grandeur. It was tired and magnificent, like a queen waiting to be crowned. Under Jessie's meticulous eye, it transformed into a palace worthy of our improbable love. Antique mirrors from forgotten estates caught the morning sun; Italian crystal chandeliers turned twilight into theatre; Persian carpets softened our steps like whispers of a well-earned peace.

It wasn't just a home. It was the story of us etched in wood and velvet, in echoes and silence. A place where two lives, once scattered, finally aligned. Where dreams stopped running, and love took root. And for a while, an exquisite, golden while it felt like life had bowed and given us our happy ending.

Sunday mornings in The Boltons moved to their own kind of time, slow, reverent, and untouched by the outside world. The city beyond the wrought-iron gates might have been spinning, but inside our home, everything was still.

The sun slipped through tall sash windows, warming the polished herringbone floors. Jessie padded barefoot through the drawing room, a linen robe tied loosely at her waist, her hair undone from the usual tight ponytail, falling in soft waves down her back. In one hand, she carried a bone china teacup. In the other, the sports section was already marked with circles and comments in her tidy, assertive scrawl.

I was in the kitchen, barefoot too, wearing a faded Oxford shirt and trying (again) to master her version of scrambled eggs, slow, patient, stirred like it was a meditation. The espresso machine hissed in approval. Somewhere in the background, Ella Fitzgerald crooned from the old record player we'd found in a Portobello stall.

"You're burning the toast again," Jessie said, leaning against the doorway, smiling like only she could, half mischief, half sunrise.

"Charred for texture," I replied, brandishing the spatula like a knight defending honour. "A bold culinary choice."

She laughed, not a loud laugh, but one that filled the room all the same. I would've burnt a hundred more slices for that sound.

We ate at the breakfast nook under the window Jessie had filled with cascading orchids. The silver was slightly tarnished, the coffee slightly bitter, but it didn't matter. In those moments, time stood still. No meetings. No matches. Just us two weary souls who had chased too much, found each other, and built a quiet kingdom where love was not loud, but certain. Outside, the world waited. But we had this. And for now, this was everything.

***

And somewhere between the relentless traveling, the endless construction projects, the dusty renovations that clung to my suits no matter how hard I tried to shake them off, and the frantic, last-minute crossings of the Channel to chase down rare pieces of forgotten furniture, there was the wedding, a luminous moment that now feels like a dream carefully stitched into the fabric of a life otherwise lived at full tilt.

It was a masterstroke of planning, executed with the flawless precision of Miss Harris, my tireless right hand, a battalion of discreet wedding planners, and, of course, Jessie herself, radiant, resolute, and somehow still calm amidst the chaos. Together, they created a day that glittered like a jewel in the heart of London, under the soaring ceilings and gilded chandeliers of The Ritz.

The guest list was a portrait of the world I had fought so hard to belong to: the "Who's Who" of the financial elite, world-renowned tennis players mingling effortlessly with high-stakes clients whose fortunes had, in some small way, been tethered to the strategies we had woven in boardrooms across continents.

Yet, as I glanced across the glittering sea of elegant gowns and tailored suits, a quiet ache threaded itself through the joy of the evening, subtle, persistent, like the ghost of a forgotten melody.

None of my schoolmates were there to raise a glass, no familiar laughs echoing from a shared childhood, no inside jokes born from creaky dormitory floors or midnight mischief. Their absence hung in the air like smoke, a soft, sorrowful reminder of a life once lived in dusty corridors and sun-bleached playgrounds.

And my family? They remained a distant echo of a door I had long since stopped knocking on. Miss Harris had tried, oh, how she had tried. She'd combed through old records, dialled long-disconnected numbers, and followed fading paper trails that led only to silence. She did it quietly, without asking, without expectation, just a hope that maybe, somewhere, someone might still be looking for me too.

But Jessie's family, warm, exuberant, unmistakably hers, had flown in from South Africa, filling the head table with laughter, Afrikaans slang, and stories that leapt across the years. They toasted, danced, and embraced as if I'd always belonged, their presence weaving a bridge between what was missing and what had miraculously appeared in its place.

For all that was absent, something beautiful had taken root. And in that moment, surrounded by music and champagne and the woman I loved, I chose to celebrate what I had, not mourn what I'd lost.

The reception unfolded like a scene from a forgotten novel, endless laughter, clinking glasses, and a kind of golden haze that wrapped itself around every memory. Someone, in an act of extraordinary generosity or sheer mischief, had managed to coax David Bowie himself into performing, and there he stood, a glittering figure, gifting the room a few unforgettable songs.

In one corner, a raucous table of Formula One drivers mimicked the sound of roaring engines with their champagne flutes, the entire section of the ballroom vibrating with the restless energy only racers possess, as if even in celebration, they couldn't sit still.

They were the same drivers who had once come knocking on the bank's doors, chasing sponsorship for their championship dreams, dreams I had believed in because I saw something familiar in them: hunger, precision, the refusal to settle.

In exchange for my faith and the bank's backing, they proudly emblazoned the National Bank's logo on their chariots of speed, taking my emblem across finish lines in Monaco, Silverstone and Suzuka.

Winners, I had thought. Just like me.

And then, as if the universe had conspired to crown the occasion, came the honeymoon, a ten-day voyage through the Mediterranean aboard a super-yacht, a lavish gesture from a client whose gratitude was almost as extravagant as the vessel itself.

I remember standing alone on the polished deck late at night, while the warm wind threaded through my hair like a familiar hand. In the distance, the lights of Monaco glittered like low-hung stars, draped carelessly along the black velvet coastline; meanwhile, at my feet, the yacht's floodlights cast a shimmering glow across the glassy water, a halo of quiet, floating light.

By day, Jessie basked in the sun on the aft deck, the black-painted hull mirrored perfectly in the still, crystalline sea. Our greatest decision each morning was which quaint seaside restaurant to choose for a romantic dinner. Meanwhile, the crew, ever attentive, endlessly patient, waited quietly on the tender, ready to ferry us ashore and back again without a word of complaint.

I would close my eyes and listen to the soft slap of water against the hull, a rhythm as ancient and dependable as breath and wonder, not without a flicker of disbelief, how a boy once abandoned at a remote boarding school on the edge of nowhere had somehow sailed into this life.

Even now, when I close my eyes, I can still hear the laughter, taste the salt on the breeze, and feel the soft, impossible weight of happiness pressing gently on my chest.

Life, against all odds, had been astonishingly, bewilderingly kind to me. And yet, even in its kindness, there lingered the faint, unshakable echo of all the things and all the people I had lost along the way.

***

The magical return from our honeymoon unfolded like the closing scene of a grand, golden romance. After a few happy years tucked away in Mayfair, life had drawn back the velvet curtain to reveal our next act: a new beginning at The Boltons.

Our new home, a stately mansion in the heart of the Boltons Conservation Area in Chelsea, was a masterful fusion of Victorian grandeur and contemporary luxury. Ornate cornices and soaring ceilings stood in perfect harmony with sleek modern finishes, creating a space that felt both timeless and entirely our own.

As always, Bill, ever the silent sentinel of our adventures, awaited us at Heathrow's arrivals hall, standing tall amid the chaotic swirl of jet-lagged travellers and lost luggage. With a subtle nod and the faintest glimmer of a smile, he whisked us away into the familiar warmth of the Rolls-Royce.

We sped through London's winter streets, the city glittering like a handful of spilled diamonds, until we reached our mansion's grand entrance and there, waiting at the top of the marble steps, was Miss Harris. Poised, immaculate, and with just the slightest conspiratorial twinkle in her eye, she stood flanked by a throng of dear friends, staff, and colleagues.

Our surprise housewarming party had been orchestrated with the precision of a royal gala: lights strung between the wrought-iron gates, the scent of fresh flowers filling the crisp night air, glasses of champagne already twinkling in gloved hands.

It was a homecoming fit for a king and queen. It was a beginning so perfect, even London itself seemed to lean in closer to watch. And as we crossed the threshold, hand in hand, into that gleaming house built on dreams, I couldn't help but feel that, for the first time in a long, long while, we were not just surviving life, we were living it.

In the golden months that followed, life unfolded with a grace so effortless it felt almost unreal, as if, just once, the universe had conspired to let the story be happy. The mansion at The Boltons became our sanctuary, a place where laughter echoed off crystal chandeliers and every sunrise whispered promises we were foolish enough to believe would last forever.

Life there often resembled a railway station, with people coming and going from every walk of life. Couriers from Harrods and Fortnum & Mason arrived daily, unloading parcels as if Christmas had been made permanent. Savile Row tailors delivered freshly pressed suits for me with reverent care, while designers floated through the front doors bearing the latest couture creations for Jessie.

There was movement, colour, joy, a rhythm to the days that felt like music. We danced through that life, she and I, without ever realising it was the overture to something fleeting. And perhaps that's what made it so perfect.

I remember once, as I descended the grand staircase on my way to the dining room, I crossed paths with a striking young woman heading up. She offered a soft smile and a breezy, "Olá."

Curious, I walked into the dining room and said to Jessie, "Who the hell is that?"

Without looking up from her tea, she replied smoothly, "That's Teresa Cortez."

"Teresa who?" I asked.

Jessie raised an eyebrow. "This year's Spanish Open champion," she said, pausing just long enough to enjoy my confusion. "You met her in New York a few years ago."

"The one with the tiny miniskirt and the barely-there top?" I asked.

Jessie grinned wickedly. "Precisely."

"She looks… different with clothes on."

"Naughty boy," she said, shaking her head but laughing all the same.

For the next few months, life flowed in a golden rhythm, a constant dance between Paternoster Square, The Boltons, and a steady stream of business trips to Spain, where I battled persistent marketing challenges like a knight fending off dragons armed only with PowerPoint slides.

Meanwhile, Jessie crisscrossed the globe with the effortless grace of a seasoned traveller: commentating at international tennis tournaments, chairing board meetings for the Tennis Association, and somehow making it all look as easy as a casual afternoon stroll.

Fast forward two years, and the world shifted once again, this time with a joyful, breathtaking surprise. Jessie, radiant with quiet excitement, announced she was pregnant with twins.

The house erupted into a frenzy of preparations, nursery renovations, the recruitment of a dedicated nanny-nurse, and endless lists drawn up with Miss Harris's surgical precision. It also marked the beginning of a quieter social season, a necessary pause from the whirl of banquets in exotic cities, holidays gifted by grateful clients, and afternoon teas in ancient castles, sipping Earl Grey alongside royalty and heads of state.

By the time the new year dawned, the final touches were complete at The Boltons. And then, on a crisp winter morning, Jessie gave birth to two beautiful, impossibly chubby twins, Francis and Paula, completing the family I had once only dared to imagine from the lonely corners of my childhood.

Professionally, life mirrored the quiet victories I was beginning to claim in my personal world. My role at the bank continued to thrive, driven by the remarkable team I had assembled, sharp, fearless, and fiercely loyal. Together, we didn't just meet targets; we redefined them. Under our leadership, the marketing division evolved into a powerhouse, strategic, agile, and consistently ahead of the curve. What once was a department fulfilling quotas became a dynamic engine of growth, innovation, and undeniable influence.

While on a business trip to the Hong Kong office, a message from Miss Harris found its way to me, brief, discreet, and electrifying:

"Sir John Nicholson, Chairman of UK Airways, is in town. He wishes to know if you would like to fly back with him to London."

It wasn't just an invitation; it was destiny in a well-tailored suit, tapping politely on the window to see if I was awake.

Moments like these don't shout; they whisper with authority. And I heard it loud and clear. I closed the file on my desk, straightened my tie, and smiled to myself.

The game had just changed.

That rainy afternoon, I boarded Sir John's private aircraft. For the next twelve hours, we carved out a deal or rather, we began the kind of dance that only men with much to gain and everything to protect know how to perform. By the time we touched down at Heathrow, The National Bank had secured the account of UK Airways, one of the largest international airlines in the world.

It was a seismic moment, not just for me but for the institution itself.

When I presented the draft memorandum of understanding at the extraordinary board meeting, the reaction was euphoric, the kind of hysterical joy usually reserved for lottery winners or peace treaties. Champagne corks flew across the boardroom like artillery shells, and for the first time, I truly felt the gravitational pull of power within my grasp.

The rewards were swift and staggering: a top promotion and a massive performance bonus. True to my lifelong promise, I directed every penny of that bonus straight into The National Bank stock options.

My dream to hold 25% of the bank, to control the empire I had once only glimpsed through the cracked windows of a boarding school dormitory, was no longer a fantasy. It was a blueprint.

At the end of that fateful month, I picked up the phone and called my old friend and faithful advisor, Gert Wessels.

Grinning ear to ear, I simply said:

"I've been appointed Head of Global Marketing Operations."

And then, after a brief, charged pause, came the message the one he knew was coming:

"Buy more shares."

I could almost see him on the other end of the line, rising to his feet, saluting with the wide, fierce grin of a man who knew deep in his bones that Gabriel Almeida was destined for banking stardom.

***

'The Times' lay neatly folded at the head of the breakfast table that August Wednesday morning. As I entered the dining room, I poured myself a black coffee, strong and unsweetened and took my usual seat, placing the paper within arm's reach.

The front page stopped me cold. A photograph of the bombed Canal Hotel in Baghdad stretched across the top, the headline announcing an attack on the United Nations headquarters. My eyes scanned the text, and my heart sank. Among the missing: Sérgio Vieira de Mello.

I left the table without touching my coffee and went directly to the sitting room. Picking up the phone, I called Miss Harris.

"Find out everything about the bombing in Baghdad, Iraq," I said, my voice flatter than I intended.

By the time I arrived at the office, Miss Harris had gathered a full account. Twenty-one dead. Among them, Sérgio. His body was recovered from beneath the rubble, nearly seven hours after the blast.

A deep, unfamiliar grief settled over me, heavy, suffocating.

"Cancel all my meetings and calls for today," I said quietly, unable to meet her eyes.

I left the building alone, walking without direction until I found myself on a bench along the Thames. There, the grey water drifted by, mirroring the stillness that had overtaken me. It was a surreal moment; for I was one of the most powerful figures in international banking, yet now just a man in mourning, unnoticed and anonymous.

Sérgio's final words to me, spoken nearly four decades ago, returned with unrelenting clarity, words I had buried deep and never dared to share:

"Pretend that none of this ever happened."

A secret I had carried in silence all these years. But the truth, like all truths, had a way of resurfacing. And with it came a weight I could no longer ignore.

The man who had quietly, invisibly shaped my life who had saved it in more ways than one, was gone. And with his death, something in me broke.

Fate had finally struck a blow I found almost impossible to bear.

For years, I told myself I was honouring his memory, protecting what he had protected, preserving the silence he had asked of me. But in doing so, I had locked away a part of myself as well. That single sentence, spoken in a low, measured voice in a room no one else remembers, had followed me through every achievement, every headline, every closed-door decision. It was both shield and shackle. I had built an entire life on truth, strategy, and integrity, and yet, the most defining moment of my past lived in shadow. And now, with Sérgio gone, I no longer knew whether I had been loyal… or simply afraid.

As I sat on that park bench overlooking the Thames, the city moved around me, joggers passing in rhythmic bursts, dogs tugging at leashes, and the faint, mournful sound of a violin drifting up from somewhere near Embankment. However, inside me, there was only stillness, the kind that doesn't calm, but presses quietly against the ribs.

I stared at my phone for a long time before pressing Glenn's name. He answered on the second ring, his voice calm and familiar, as if no time had passed.

"You alright, Gabe?" he asked, picking up on something in my silence. He always did.

"I need to tell you something," I said. "Something I should've told you years ago."

There was a pause on the other end. Not surprised. Just waiting.

"Sérgio gave me an instruction," I continued. "Right after I was released. Just one sentence: 'Pretend that none of this ever happened.'"

Another pause, but this time, it was heavier.

"For forty years I've carried it," I said. "Protected it. Protected him. But it changed me, Glenn. It shaped everything. And now… I don't know what to do with it. He's gone. The world's moved on. But I haven't."

Glenn was quiet for a moment, and then his voice softened. "Maybe it's not about protecting the past anymore," he said. "Maybe it's about setting yourself free from it."

The words settled over me like dusk.

"I didn't realise how heavy it had become," I said.

"You do now," Glenn replied gently. "And maybe that's enough."

Four days later, I stood alone in a crowd of mourners at Sérgio's funeral in Brazil, where the air was dense not just with heat, but with grief so palpable it felt woven into every breath. This wasn't just my sorrow; it belonged to the world, as heads of state, seasoned diplomats, humanitarians, journalists, and friends from every corner of the globe had gathered to honour him. Some arrived in armoured convoys while others came quietly on foot, but all bore the same expression: one of stunned reverence, of having lost someone irreplaceable.

The ceremony unfolded beneath a grey sky that refused to rain, as though even the heavens were holding their breath. I watched from the edge, a solitary figure among dignitaries and world figures, clutching memories far too private for the grandeur of the setting. No eulogy could capture the depth of what he had given, not just to nations, but to individuals like me. And in that crowd, amidst cameras and protocol, I felt the weight of silence more than any anthem or speech. And then came the tribute from Kofi Annan, steady, dignified, final:

"The entire United Nations family is grieving. We have lost one of our finest colleagues. Sérgio was a man of courage, dedication, and compassion. The world is a darker place without him."

Those words etched themselves into me, more lasting than marble, more permanent than any gravestone. They would stay with me for the rest of my life.

And then, one of the mourners made a passing reference to the TWA hijacking in Beirut and how Sérgio had been instrumental in achieving a peaceful outcome.

Suddenly, something inside me shifted. A memory, long buried, rose to the surface: my hush-hush return to Cape Town after the hijacking… Richard Campbell's wife, the former UN advisor… and, of course, the man in the white suit standing on the airport's viewing platform just before I boarded the plane, the smile, the slow wave goodbye.

It hadn't been a stranger.

It was Sérgio.

My invisible saviour.

Chapter 16:
Ambition Delivered; Love Taken.

My position had brought me ever closer to the Executive Board, a seat at the table I had long set my sights on. I set myself a clear goal: to achieve that position before my sixtieth birthday. And for the first time, it felt not just possible, but inevitable.

But ambition rarely comes without cost. The demands of the role, particularly the travel involve sacrifices, many of them subtle, but some more deeply felt.

Though I was able to delegate much of the international travel to trusted senior members of my team, there were times when only my presence could resolve a crisis. And so, I kept going, troubleshooting across continents, smoothing complications in far-off boardrooms.

On more than one occasion, as the executive jet touched down at Heathrow after another whirlwind trip, I found myself staring out at the rain-slicked tarmac, unsure whether I'd taken off from Shanghai… or Singapore… or somewhere in between.

At first, the distance felt manageable, measured in-flight hours and calendar entries, nothing that couldn't be offset with a weekend at home or an extravagant family holiday. But slowly, almost imperceptibly, it began to stretch. I would return from trips to find the twins taller, their interests shifting, inside jokes passing over my head like headlines I hadn't read. Jessie, ever composed, never complained, but there was a quiet in her eyes sometimes, a subtle pause in conversation, as if she were waiting for me to notice something I no longer had the time to see.

One evening, I arrived home earlier than expected. The house was bathed in golden lamplight, soft jazz drifting through the hallway like a memory trying to find its way back. I found Jessie curled up on the sofa, a novel open on her lap, but her eyes unfocused, watching the twins from across the room. Francis was explaining something animatedly to Paula, both of them laughing in a way that felt like a language I no longer spoke. Jessie looked up when she saw me. She smiled, genuinely, but there was a flicker in her expression, something like surprise. As if she had forgotten, just for a moment, that I lived there too.

The constant travel was wearing down more than just my body; it was quietly eroding the foundation of my family. Somewhere between connecting flights and closed-door meetings, my priorities had shifted. What once felt like ambition began to feel like absence. And with that shift came a quiet, insistent truth: no boardroom, no quarterly target, no title embossed on a glass door was worth losing the people I loved most.

So, I enforced what Jessie called a "corporate ceasefire," an extended family holiday designed to make up for the years of absence and half-heard stories told over rushed dinners.

The Pacific Islands became our playground for over a month. We travelled with an entourage expansive enough to make royalty blush, chefs, tutors, a personal medic, a team of discreet security ensuring that nothing was out of reach, and nothing interrupted our time together.

Gone were the board meetings, the strategic briefings, the endless client dinners. In their place: sunrises over turquoise waters, lazy breakfasts, laughter without agenda. For the first time in years, I wasn't the Head of Global Marketing Operations. I was just Gabriel. Husband. Father. Present.

When we finally returned to The Boltons, I felt renewed calm, centred, even hopeful. But with the peace came a question I could no longer avoid: was it time to slow down?

The twins were preparing for university at Exeter. Jessie, ever graceful, never asked for anything, but I could see in her eyes the desire for permanence, for presence.

And yet…

After a long, silent conversation with myself, the kind only ambition understands, the answer came, sharp and clear.

Of course not.

What about the Executive Board? What about the CEO seat or higher still, Chairman of The National Bank?

That was the dream.

That had always been the goal.

***

Sitting in the back of the Rolls-Royce on a cold winter's morning, Bill steady at the wheel and the Financial Times folded beside me, I reached for the phone.

"Miss Harris," I said, "schedule a call with Glenn Smith. Today."

Glenn, my old schoolmate, trusted advisor and quiet mentor. Of all the people in my life, he remained the one person I could speak to without pretence. No performance. No filters. Just truth.

I had a scheduled trip to South Africa and arranged to meet him while I was there. There were questions I needed to ask, questions that had been circling in my mind for weeks and answers I knew only Glenn could help me find.

Should I walk away now?

Should I leave it all behind, the ambition, the climb, the long-promised seat at the top, and not achieve the goal I had chased for most of my life?

That same morning, upon arriving at the bank just as I was finishing a long, thoughtful call with Glenn, a surprise invitation landed on my desk. Sir Godfrey himself had summoned me to lunch at Claridge's in Mayfair. And when the eighty-year-old Chairman of the Board invites you to lunch, you don't check your diary. You stand up. You go. It's not the sort of offer one refuses.

I arrived promptly at 1:00 p.m., crossing the marbled, checkerboard lobby beneath the glittering chandelier, into the dining room that whispered quiet opulence with every step. I took my seat and waited for the man who had once defined the institution I now helped run.

The greetings were warm, even affectionate and included, at his insistence, a detailed account of our recent Pacific holiday.

Then, just as we were tucking into our lobster Thermidor, the tone shifted.

It began with the usual preamble: my four decades of service, my contribution to the bank's meteoric rise, the example I had set for both staff and shareholders. All of it felt rehearsed. Familiar. And then:

Without a hint of ceremony, Sir Godfrey set down his glass, looked me dead in the eye, and said: "I'm stepping down. I want you to take over."

I froze. The moment landed like a thunderclap in an empty room. My dream, the one whispered into a dormitory mattress, nurtured through boardrooms and battles, wins and wounds, had finally come true.

We left Claridge's hours later, fuelled by champagne and mutual respect. As I walked across Green Park toward the banks of the Thames, a strange numbness settled over me, not fear, not disbelief, but the stillness that follows the collision of destiny and reality.

I found myself daydreaming, tracing time backward to the boy with a few hidden cents tucked behind his bedframe in a South African boarding school. A secret savings stash. A beginning.

A story only ever shared with my closest family… and, in quiet moments of encouragement, with the girls, reminders that great things start small, and that even the boldest futures can begin in silence.

The morning after Claridge's, I sat by the window at The Boltons, the offer still echoing in my mind like the last note of a grand symphony. The title I had chased for most of my life, the chairmanship of the National Bank, was within reach. And yet, amid the quiet triumph, a strange heaviness settled in my chest. Of all the people I wished could have witnessed this moment, it was Sérgio Vieira de Mello, who lingered most in my thoughts. He had shaped my path more than he ever knew, his quiet diplomacy, his belief in human resilience, the letter he never wrote but always lived by. He was the first man of consequence who saw something in me when the world still only saw a boy behind enemy lines. I often wondered what he would have said, had he been across the table at Claridge's, raising a glass not just to my title, but to the journey.

Perhaps just a smile, subtle, knowing.

The kind that needed no words.

***

With Sir Godfrey's proposal still echoing in my head like a forgotten ringtone in a silent library, I stepped out into the kind of spring morning that made even the pigeons look smug. The air was crisp, infused with the scent of cut grass, early blossoms, and the faint whiff of privilege. A platoon of street sweepers advanced down the pavement with the solemn precision of a military parade, each wielding a broom as if auditioning for the Royal Ballet of Sanitation. The towering plane trees that lined The Boltons stood like judgmental aunts at a christening, nodding slightly in the breeze, as if to say, 'You've still not dealt with that Godfrey nonsense, have you?'

Back at home, Ms Dwyer, our housekeeper of over two decades and the undisputed matriarch of all things domestic, was already preparing breakfast with the controlled intensity of a Michelin chef disarming a soufflé. She ran the house with an iron fist wrapped in a floral oven mitt, and though she claimed to be "just keeping busy," we all knew MI5 had nothing on her surveillance network.

The garden room table was set with the kind of precision that made one suspect Ms Dwyer had used a spirit level. It awaited Jessie, the twins, Mr and Mrs Parker (who spoke mostly in italicised whispers), and a handful of cousins visiting from South Africa, each one more eccentric than the last. One had arrived with a suitcase full of biltong and the firm belief that London traffic lights were optional.

Our home, over the years, had become something of a diplomatic outpost disguised as a family residence, a curious crossroads where tennis champions, second cousins twice removed, and the occasional South American film producer with a questionable visa all somehow converged. I often suspected there was an invisible sign outside reading:

"Strays Welcome, Just Don't Touch the China."

Later that morning, as tradition (and Ms Dwyer's glare) dictated, we trooped off to the Hurlingham Club, that verdant fortress of exclusivity nestled along the Thames, where power wore pastel and influence arrived in Jaguars that hadn't depreciated since 1963. The air buzzed with wealth, tennis balls, and the faint scent of expensive regret.

That afternoon, the club was hosting its annual Concours d'Elegance, a celebration of automotive beauty and middle-aged men casually weeping over carburettors. Several of my racing driver friends were in attendance, their vintage automobiles gleaming like Fabergé eggs on wheels. I spotted Nigel, proudly polishing a Bugatti that looked like it had been restored with the tears of Italian artisans.

It was a day that shimmered with effortless perfection, golden, glossy, and ever so slightly smug.

And yet, as the sun dipped behind the clubhouse roof and the champagne fizzed into silence, a curious disquiet settled in my chest. A whisper of unease. The kind of feeling you get when someone compliments your shoes, then asks if you've been limping. Something, somewhere, was shifting and not just the gears in Nigel's Bugatti.

***

I was slowly coming to terms with Sérgio's untimely death, almost three months had passed, when, after yet another evening entertaining clients at White's, the exclusive gentlemen's club in St. James's, I returned home and began packing for my next business trip.

By midmorning, Bill had arrived, the Rolls idling in the driveway as I zipped the final corner of my suitcase. Destination: Heathrow. Another long-haul flight to Hong Kong. Another deal to close.

As Jessie stood in the doorway, waving goodbye, I hesitated for a beat longer than usual. There was a weight in my chest, not panic, not dread, just a quiet unease. A voice I couldn't quite hear but also couldn't ignore.

You should have rescheduled, it said. *Stay home. Be with them.*

But instead, I smiled, waved back, and closed the car door.

Jessie was scheduled to collect the twins from Exeter the next morning. I should've been there waiting at the gates, arms open, ready to hear their stories tumbling out in excited bursts. But once again, I had chosen boardrooms over bedtime stories, strategy over presence. My relentless pursuit of success had clouded the moments that truly mattered. And as I stared in silence at our home and the woman I loved standing on the doorway, I couldn't shake the fear that this wouldn't be the last time I let them down.

The British Airways flight touched down at Hong Kong International Airport late that morning. By the time I arrived at the hotel and checked in, I reached for my phone and called Jessie, just as we'd agreed.

The call went unanswered. That alone was unusual. But it wasn't just one missed call. I rang again. And again. Still nothing. That's when the first wave of dread began to rise slowly, cold, and merciless. Something was wrong. I didn't know what. But I knew.

Panic overtook me. In a frantic rush, I called Miss Harris once, twice, over and over, each unanswered ring another weight pressing against my chest.

And then, the phone rang.

Miss Harris. Her voice was composed but thick with emotion.

"There's been a terrible accident," she said. Then a pause. "Jessie and the girls… Please return as soon as possible."

She went on to explain that she had already summoned the company's private jet to bring me home without delay.

I pressed for more details, facts. Something to hold onto. But there was nothing more she could say.

Bill was waiting at Heathrow. We drove in silence back to The Boltons.

Mr and Mrs Parker stood at the front steps, their faces pale and drawn, as if the words they were about to speak had already broken them.

"There was an accident," they said, and then after a long, unbearable pause, "They didn't survive."

My world shattered.

Another blow. But not just another.

The blow. The one I would never recover from.

I didn't walk, I staggered, propelled by something raw and primal, the weight of disbelief pressing against my chest like a stone. I reached the bedroom, our bedroom, and collapsed onto the bed, the same bed where laughter had once lived, where whispered promises were made in the hush of night, where Jessie had often fallen asleep with her hand curled in mine as if anchoring us both to something real.

Her scent was still there, delicate but undeniable lavender, sandalwood, and something uniquely her. It clung to the pillows, to the folds of the duvet, to the very air, like an echo refusing to fade. I pressed my face into the fabric, searching for her in cotton and memory, willing time to fold back on itself.

The curtains were drawn, casting the room in a gentle, sepia gloom. Shadows stretched along the walls like long, silent prayers. Then, without warning, the domed light on Jessie's dressing table flicked on soft, golden, and steady.

It stopped me cold.

That light, her light, glowed as if summoned by something beyond logic. Not the flick of a switch, but the flicker of something eternal.

For one impossible, aching moment, I believed it was her. Her way of reaching through the the veil, her whisper in the silence, her strength, cradling my broken heart.

I'm okay. Be strong, my darling.

And in that fragile illusion, I broke.

Tears spilled freely, hot and unrelenting, soaking the sheets as grief poured out in breathless sobs. I held the pillow to my chest as it could somehow bring her back, like it might hold the shape of her one last time.

There was no body to bury yet, nor a grave to visit. Just this room, our sacred little universe now a mausoleum of touch, scent, and silence.

And so, I clung to what I had left. Not her body. But her presence. Her memory. Her light. Her love.

Because in that moment, it was all I had.

And somehow, it had to be enough

***

The tragic accident dominated headlines across newspapers and television channels: *"Wife and Daughters of Prominent Banker Killed in Fatal Crash."*

The in-depth reports revealed the details with cold precision.

A head-on collision between a Range Rover and a British Army MAN support truck had occurred along the picturesque A303, at the junction with Allington Track. According to early investigations, the vehicle driven by Mrs Jessie Almeida had lost control after skidding on a patch of black ice.

Jessie, a renowned professional tennis player and commentator, had been returning home with her twin daughters for a long-awaited family reunion ahead of Christmas.

None of the occupants survived.

I sat motionless in front of the television, the images flickering across the screen like scenes from someone else's life. Photos of Jessie in her prime, smiling after a match, laughing beside the twins now framed in sorrowful montages, narrated by voices that spoke with polished sympathy but knew nothing of the woman, or the life, we had shared.

Newspapers lay scattered across the dining table, each one bearing the same awful truth, dressed in bold type and polished language. They spoke of loss, of tragedy, of ice and timing and fate, but none of them captured the silence that had settled in our home, the hollow ache that pressed into my ribs with every breath.

My grief was no longer mine alone. It belonged to the world, now dissected, published, consumed. And yet, none of it brought them back.

That evening, after the calls had stopped and the house had settled into a heavy, unnatural stillness, I climbed the stairs alone. Each step creaked beneath my feet, the sound stretched thin by grief, like the ticking of a clock winding down. It wasn't just the ascent of a staircase. It was the slow rise into a different kind of life, one I hadn't asked for. One without them.

I paused outside the twins' bedroom, my hand resting on the doorknob and trembling slightly. My heart thudded in my chest. not fast, just... heavy, as if I were about to cross a threshold between memory and aftermath, and between what was and what would never be again. It felt both sacred and cruel, like entering a cathedral where the gods had gone silent.

Inside, everything was as they'd left it, untouched by tragedy, unaware. The desks still bore open textbooks mid-sentence, questions unanswered, dreams still inked into the margins. A hoodie lay draped across the back of a chair, one sleeve dangling as if waiting to be tugged on. A pair of sneakers sat obediently by the bed, laces undone, ready for a tomorrow that would never come. The air smelled faintly of sunblock and lavender shampoo, mixed with something unmistakably theirs, a warm, sugary scent I could never quite name but would know anywhere.

I lowered myself to the floor. Not crying. Not yet. Just breathing slow, shallow breaths that barely stirred the quiet around me. My hands rested in my lap, empty and useless. I wasn't ready to grieve. I wasn't ready to accept. I was simply trying to remember how to exist in a world they no longer touched.

And for the first time since the news, I realised: absence wasn't silence. It was deafening. And it lived in every corner of this room.

There was no eulogy yet. No speech prepared. Just this: a father in an empty room, quietly breaking.

The church service was held on a bitterly cold morning, at the very same chapel where Jessie and I had been married twenty-five years earlier. There was a cruel symmetry to it, love and loss echoing beneath the same vaulted ceiling, in the same pews where joy had once lived.

It was a private ceremony, quiet and dignified, attended only by close friends and family. Afterwards, we made our way to the burial at Mill Hill Cemetery, just as a gentle blanket of snow began to fall, soft, unhurried, and achingly beautiful.

The congregation, small but loyal, stood in silence as the earth received what my heart could not let go of. And for a moment, the world felt suspended, hushed under white, as if even the sky had bowed its head.

Long after the others had drifted away, their condolences offered, their scarves drawn tighter against the cold, I remained at the graveside, frozen in place, not by the weather, but by the weight of it all.

The snow continued to fall, softening the outlines of everything, headstones, trees, even memory. I stared at the mound of earth, not knowing what to say, because everything I wanted to tell them, Jessie, Francis, and Paula felt too small. Too late.

I should have been there. I should have changed my flight.

I should have listened to the voice that told me not to go.

But guilt is a quiet tyrant. It doesn't rage, it just settles in your bones, one breath at a time.

And as I stood there, hands clenched in my coat pockets, I realised something that cut deeper than the grief itself:

They were no longer part of the world. But I was.

And I had no idea how to live in it without them.

Chapter 17:
And Then There Was Silence.

It took me months to return to the office. Life as it once was no longer held meaning. I drifted through the days like a man half-awake. Andy J Clark, the fashion magnate and longtime friend, invited me on a cruise through the Caribbean, hoping a change of scenery might bring some light back into my eyes. However, as we sailed across, still, perfect waters, my heart remained somewhere else, frozen in the silence I carried with me.

A deep depression settled over me, and for the first time in my life, my doctors grew seriously concerned about my well-being. I had scaled the heights of wealth and success, but suddenly it meant nothing. Without my family, without Sérgio, whose influence had helped shape the empire I built, money had lost its meaning.

When I finally returned to London, I summoned two of the people I trusted most: Gerald King, my solicitor of thirty years, and Gert Wessels, my friend and confidant, now the bank's Chief Financial Officer. We met at White's for what became a long, quiet conversation, part legal briefing, part confession, part farewell. In the space of four hours, I mapped out my future.

It felt less like a financial strategy and more like the writing of a last will and testament. The shares I had painstakingly acquired in the bank, now worth millions, would be sold and divided equally among those who had shaped my life when I had nothing: Monica, Glenn, Candice, the twins Pieter and Willem, and Hendrik.

The remainder of my estate, my properties, investments, and private holdings would be liquidated. The proceeds were donated in full to the Twinn Foundation and to Glenn's alma mater, now renamed the University of Good Hope, in honour of the grace and second chances that had once found me in the unlikeliest of places.

Walking away from the bank, from the gleaming boardrooms, the limelight, the empire I had once dreamed of owning, felt nothing like I imagined it would. There was no ceremony, no farewell toast or golden send-off. Just a signature, a handshake, and a silence that felt more liberating than any applause. For years, I had chased that corner office, that chair at the head of the table. But in the end, it meant nothing without the voices I had hoped to share it with.

And so, I returned home.

Not to The Boltons or Mayfair, nor to the glass towers and marble corridors of Paternoster Square, where ambition wore a sharp suit and time was measured in closing bells and quarterly reports. No, I returned to where it had all begun. To the red earth and thorn trees. To a land that had both scarred me and shaped me. I came back to South Africa not as the man I had once dreamed of becoming, but as the man life had carved from the stone of experience.

When I arrived in Barberton, the past met me like an old friend. I carried nothing but a small suitcase and a lifetime's worth of memories, folded and worn like the clothes I packed. The Impala Hotel still stood proudly, though time had softened its edges. I checked in quietly, no fanfare. Just me and the whispers of yesterycars. It was here I prepared for a reunion long overdue with the friends who had carried my spirit when my legs could not. The boys who had become my brothers.

Together, we walked again through the gates of our old school. Once, they'd felt like bars, holding back the boy I used to be. Now, they opened like arms, welcoming and familiar, and as we stood side by side, older, greyer, but no less bonded, I realised the power of those early years. That institution had broken me, yes, but it had also built me. It had given me the people who taught me how to fight, how to rise, and above all, how to feel loved.

I had come full circle. Back to the ochre soil and vast skies. To the haunting silence of the veldt at dusk and the first calls of the hadeda at dawn. Back to the laughter echoing across dormitory halls and the smell of chalk and varnished wood. Back to the place that had taught me how to survive… and to the people who had shown me how to live.

The road ahead was quieter now, stripped of titles and boardrooms, of champagne galas and airport lounges. My days were no longer marked by agendas, only by sunrises, soft conversations, and the scent of jacaranda in bloom.

And in that quiet, in the slow, deliberate rhythm of a simpler life, I finally found what had eluded me through decades of running, building and climbing.

Peace.

www.ingramcontent.com/pod-product-compliance
Lightning Source LLC
Chambersburg PA
CBHW071616030726
47598CB00001B/299